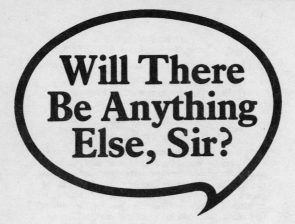

Will There Be Anything Else, Sir?

Maurice Lautman

ARROW BOOKS

Arrow Books Limited
17–21 Conway Street, London W1P 6JD

An imprint of the Hutchinson Publishing Group

London Melbourne Sydney Auckland
Johannesburg and agencies throughout
the world

First published 1984

Set in Linoterm Plantin
by JH Graphics Limited, Reading

Printed and bound in Great Britain
by Anchor Brendon Limited, Tiptree, Essex

ISBN 0 09 937000 X

Contents

This book is dedicated to my dear wife and daughter, Edna and Louise, and to the memory of my dear late brother Sam who is sadly missed.

With grateful thanks for their help to Richard Evans, Faith Brooker and Jeremy Tzen.

Hello There, Come On In . . .

Now what can I do for you? In need of a brush up or just looked in to get out of the rain? Well, it's good to see you anyway, even if you look a bit grey around the gills. Perhaps I can recommend a tonic? Something to restore your natural shine and bring back a bit of bounce to your life. May I suggest that you're bored with all those westerns and hospital romances that pack the shelves this time of year? That you no longer care who shot the sheriff or if the night nurse is torn between the demands of her career and the attentions of the senior intern's stethoscope? And wouldn't you prefer a book that makes you laugh for a change rather than one of the crime or horror novels that will keep you up all night wondering just what that strange shadow is doing behind the wardrobe or if the blood-curdling noise you hear next door is really their youngest son's latest attempt to learn the saxophone or in fact an unholy sacrificial orgy of gruesome proportions? If you're with me so far, then come on in and have a browse – you won't find anything to make you weep or scream in here – except with laughter, of course! Sit back and enjoy the couple of hundred jokes or so that I and my brothers gathered together over our years in the barber shop. I tell you, there's not much we didn't find to laugh about, because there's not much that people won't talk about when they're comfortably relaxed in the barber's chair with the chance of a good gossip and exchanging a gag or two.

You see, the hairdresser's used to be more than just a place to go when you needed a short back and sides or a blue-rinse and a back-comb – it was as much a centre of the community as the local pub – somewhere you could always find someone to listen to you and to swap stories with. Our job was to entertain and set our customers at ease, to provide a short respite from the world outside – to cheer them up as well as to make them look better, and no one looks better than when they've got a smile on their face, do they?

So when I was asked to put *Will There Be Anything Else, Sir?* together, it was with the atmosphere of the old barber's shop in mind, with the added pleasure of knowing that the jokes and stories between its pages would be reaching even more chuckle-needy customers than ever before. I hope you'll enjoy curling up with the selection – whatever your style, there should be something to suit everyone in here – so, are you sitting comfortably? Then I'll begin . . .

I
Hair There and Everywhere

(A barber's lot)

9

I was telling one of my hairdresser rivals, a surly bloke, about the holiday I'd recently spent in Japan.

'Funny,' said my rival, 'I'm going to Japan next week for a holiday myself.'

'Well,' I said, 'whatever you do, don't come back unless you've had the wax treatment.'

'The wax treatment?' said the man. 'What on earth's that?'

But I refused to tell him. My rival, a jealous man, didn't want to miss out on anything I'd tried, so when he arrived in Japan, he wandered the streets of Tokyo until he saw a sign saying WAX TREATMENT GIVEN HERE.

He went inside and was greeted by a beautiful Japanese girl, who stripped him naked, laid him down on his back and rubbed oil into his body.

'What next?' he whispered huskily to the girl.

'HIROHITO!' she shouted.

At her cry, a huge Japanese wrestler rushed into the room with a club and hit him so hard on his dick that all the wax came out of his ears.

An apprentice barber was doing a very bad job of shaving a customer. When he'd finished, he asked the customer, 'Did you come in with a red tie?'

'No,' said the customer.

'Oh dear,' said the assistant. 'Well, you're going out with one.'

Another of my rivals would say anything to make his money up . . .

As he was shaving a customer, the barber let out an enormous sigh.

'What is it, Sid?' said the customer, 'You sound pretty fed up.'

'I was just thinking of my poor twin brother Eddie. He went mad, you know.'

'Went mad? Good lord, I had no idea. What on earth happened?'

'Well, you know, there's no money in this business unless a customer has a shampoo as well as a shave. He was going bankrupt and it must have sent him loony. I caught him trying to cut a customer's throat because he refused a shampoo – that's why I had to have him put away. Sometimes I wish I'd let him slash away – it might have saved his sanity. By the way, sir, did you say shampoo?'

'Yes, *please*!!'

A man went into a barber's shop for a haircut and sat down in the chair.

'How do you want your hair done?' said the barber.

'My wife likes it long and thick,' said the customer.

'So does mine,' said the barber, 'but how do you want your hair cut?'

Barber: How are things going, Mr Stevenson?

Mr S: Hectic, George, hectic. In fact I'm off to the country this weekend for a bit of peace and quiet.

Barber: Nothing like a little peace, sir.

Mr S: No, indeed, George. Let's just hope she keeps quiet.

A barber was shaving a man one day when the man said, 'Have you got a spare razor?'

'Why?' asked the barber.

'I want to defend myself.'

A barber won £250,000 on the pools.

'What are we going to do about all the begging letters?' asked his wife.

'Well,' said the barber, 'keep sending them, I suppose.'

A Greek barber was annoyed when a Chinese man opened a restaurant opposite his shop. Every time he saw the restaurant owner on the street he would cry:

'Flied lice, flied lice, Chinaman.'

The Chinese man became angry with this continual insult, so he went to elocution lessons, and learned to say 'Fried rice' perfectly. When he next saw the Greek barber he received the usual taunt:

'Flied lice, flied lice, Chinaman.'

The Chinaman turned calmly and looked the Greek in the eye.

'Fried rice, fried rice,' he said, 'you Gleek plick.'

One summer it was so hot that we opened up the back yard and shaved the customers in the open air. It was a great success, but one day, when my mother-in-law was visiting the shop, a friend popped his head round and said: 'Oh! Do you shave on the outside?'

To which my mother-in-law retorted: 'What d'you think? That he's fur-lined?'

Sign outside barbers:
WE NEED YOUR HEAD IN OUR BUSINESS!

A man opened the door of a barber's shop and said to the barber, 'How long will you be?'

'About an hour,' replied the barber.

'I'll come back,' said the man. But he didn't return until the following day, and when he did, he asked the same question. 'How long will you be?'

'About an hour,' said the barber again.

'I'll come back.'

Again he didn't return until the following day, and the same thing happened. This went on all week until finally the barber told his assistant to follow the man and see where he went.

When the assistant returned, the barber said, 'Well, where did he go?'

'Straight round to your house,' said the boy.

A man went into a barber's shop and sat down in the chair.

'I'd like a Tony Curtis, please,' he said to the barber.

The barber started to shave off all the man's hair.

'Hang on,' said the customer. 'I said a Tony Curtis!'

'Just relax, sir,' said the barber. 'I know what I'm doing.'

He proceeded to shear the man's hair until he was completely bald.

'I wanted a Tony Curtis!' said the enraged customer.

'Look,' said the barber, 'you don't have to tell me – I saw *The King and I* three times.'

After having what was left of his hair trimmed, a nearly bald customer asked the barber how much he owed him.

'Three quid,' said the barber.

'Three quid!' replied the customer indignantly, 'That's more than you charge some people with a full head of hair!'

'That's right,' said the barber. 'A treasure-hunt costs more.'

Time flies . . .

A fly and his grandson were walking on top of a bald man's head, when the old fly turned to the young one and said: 'You know son, I remember when this was just a footpath.'

If barristers can be de-barred, ministers can be de-frocked, can hair-dressers be dis-tressed?

Customer to barber: 'What hairstyles have you got?'

'We've got a Yul Brynner, a Tony Curtis and a Tom Jones.'

'I'll have a Tom Jones.'

The hairdresser proceeded to shear away all his hair.

'That's not a Tom Jones,' said the furious customer.

'It is when you come in here,' said the barber.

A man was having a shave in a barber's. At the same time he was enjoying a manicure from a very attractive female assistant. He took a fancy to the girl and decided to try his luck. 'You're a very

13

lovely young girl,' he said. 'How would you like to have dinner with me, see a show, and come back to my place afterwards?'

'Oh,' she said, 'I don't think my husband would like that.'

'Oh come on,' said the man. 'How would he know?'

'Because he's the one who's shaving you.'

After having his hair cut, a hairdresser showed a customer the back of his hair in a mirror.

'I asked you for a Tony Curtis,' said the customer, 'and you've given me a Robert Powell.'

'What do you mean, a Robert Powell?' asked the barber.

'See for yourself,' said the furious customer. 'It's got thirty-nine steps.'

I couldn't help overhearing a conversation in a pub some time ago, concerning a friend of mine called Smith.

First man: Smith says he's in close touch with the heads of several big concerns.

Second man: Oh, he's always boasting. That's probably not true at all.

Me: Excuse me, but it's true all right. Smith's a barber!

A barber had two razors, one large and one small. One morning he was trying to shave a customer with the big razor, when he realized that it was far too blunt. As his little boy was in the shop, his father told him to go and get the baby razor. Running to the bottom of the stairs, the little chap looked up and shouted:

'Mum, dad wants you!'

Kids often make you smile with the things they come out with. Take little Jennifer for instance . . .

Jennifer: Mummy, you're very naughty – you sent me to the hairdresser's with a dirty neck!

Mrs Brown: Of course I didn't Jennifer. What are you talking about?

Jennifer: Well, I know it was dirty, 'cause he used the vacuum cleaner on it!

A nervous assistant was giving his first shave to a one-armed man. The boy shaved him very badly, cutting the customer's face in several places. Eventually, having been told that small talk relaxes the customer, he asked, 'Er, have you been here before, sir?'

'No,' replied the man acidly. 'I lost this arm in the war.'

Two men were waiting in the barber's, one white and one black. The white man asked the barber for a Telly Savalas.

'OK,' said the barber. 'That'll be twelve pounds.'

Next it was the black man's turn.

'I'd like a Telly Savalas as well,' he said.

The barber shaved his head, and said it would be £46.

'Forty-six pounds?' said the black man. 'You only charged the other guy twelve.'

'Ah yes,' said the barber, 'but it's always more for a coloured telly.'

A sign outside a barber's shop said: COME IN TOMORROW FOR FREE HAIRCUT.

Fred saw it, went back the next day and asked for his free haircut.

'Can't you read?' said the barber. 'It says come back tomorrow!'

Before he went on holiday, Joe, an affable chap, was getting his hair cut by a barber known for his sour disposition.

'And where are you going on holiday then, Joe?' said the barber.

'Oh!' said Joe. 'I'm so excited! It'll be the holiday of a lifetime – this year we'll be doing the whole tour: France, Spain, Germany, and the route we'll be taking will end up in Italy, where we're going to try to get an audience with the Pope!'

The barber was unimpressed. 'Oh yeah,' he said. 'Well I hope you've heard about the terrible weather they're having in France – seems it's due to go on for another month or so. Myself, I can't stand the French, or that winey muck they pass off as food – frogs' legs and snails seems a funny diet to me. As for the Spanish I hear they're having some trouble with the water there – I've never trusted that or the air abroad myself – and I should take some stuff for gyppy tummy if you plan to eat any of the oily rubbish they'll give you in the hotel – if it's built by then, of course, which would be a novelty. I must admit I'm surprised you're bothering with Germany – everyone knows the food's dreadful and you'll never get a decent pint of beer unless you go for that detergent they dish up in gerry-cans. Besides which you'll have to put up with the Germans – who are probably the rudest, most inhospitable people on the face of the earth (apart from the French of course) and anyway who won the war, eh?

Still, if you're ending up in Italy, I should watch out you don't get kidnapped by terrorists and ransomed for whatever fortune you have left after squandering it on rubbishy over-priced souvenirs from half of Europe – that's if you're still moving about after all that greasy food, of course. And what did you say? An audience with the Pope? You'll be lucky! That man's not interested in the likes of you and me – you'll think yourself privileged if you manage to catch his eye from the back of the crowd in St Peter's Square! If I was you, I'd stay at home – you'll save your money, and at least you'll get a decent cup of tea!'

Somewhat taken aback by all this, Joe paid for his haircut and promptly left the shop. A month went by, and Joe duly returned. As he sat down in the chair, the barber said, 'Well, sir, what did I tell you? Have a pretty rough time I should say from the look of you.'

'Well, actually,' said Joe, 'you couldn't have been more wrong. When we got to France, the weather was wonderful, so hot that we spent most of the time wearing shorts and T-shirts. When we got to Paris, my wife was thrilled – the hotel management found out it was her birthday and sent a complimentary meal up to our room with flowers and champagne – all on the house, can you believe it! And the food was wonderful, beautiful steaks that melted in your mouth, fresh salads and, actually, I tried snails and thought they were delicious! In Spain we went swimming every day in the hotel's pool – though the rooms were so luxurious it was a pity to leave them for the outside sunshine. We ate seafood every day and fresh fruit the size of which I'd never thought possible. But I think the Germans were the nicest, most helpful people we met. In the hotel there, I got friendly with the manager and he invited us for a weekend in the mountains, where they were holding a drinking contest – when I won, he gave me an open invite to go back and stay with him and his wife any time, for as long as we liked – the beer was delicious, too! But the highlight of the holiday was really when we got to Rome. What a city! And the people were so nice to us. We were on a shopping excursion one day, and as we walked through the doors of this big apartment store, we got showered with roses and my wife was presented with an enormous box of chocolates – evidently we were their one millionth customer, and could have anything in the store that we could carry away – it was fantastic – the wife got a fur coat, I got some terrific suits and a new watch among other things, but when the manager was taking us round, and asked me what I'd like more than anything else in the whole world, I joked, "You couldn't get us an audience with the Pope, could you?" It was incredible. It turned out that he was the son of one of the Pope's personal secretaries, and he said he would do whatever he could. I didn't think much more about it, but the next day, we got a card with a purple border, requesting our presence at the Vatican that afternoon!'

'So you got in to see the Pope?' said the barber, weakly.

'Yes!' said Joe. 'I was very nervous at first, but he really is a wonderful man. In no time at all we were chatting like old buddies – he was so interested in everything – what I did for a living, where I lived, what I thought about politics – everything. It was as if I'd known him all my life. Anyway, the time came to go, and before I left, I asked if he would give me a blessing. He said that he would be delighted to do so, and as I knelt in front of him, and he placed his hand on my head, he said the thing I shall never forget to my dying day.'

'What did he say?' asked the barber.

'Who the bloody hell cut your hair?!'

Stan Cox was looking for his brother, Bob. He couldn't find him in any of his usual pubs, so he tried the barber's shop, thinking that he might be having a shave.

'Bob Cox here?' he called out to me.

'Sorry, sir,' I said, 'We only do haircuts and shaves.'

I once had an apprentice barber called Michael – and he used to send me up the wall. I once went with him to the cinema, and after I'd bought my ticket, I went in expecting him to follow me. After ten minutes or so I went looking for the boy, only to discover him still outside at the cashier's desk.

'Cor, bloody expensive, this,' he said.

The cashier looked at me and said, 'It's the sixth ticket he's bought.'

'Michael,' I said. 'Why do you keep buying tickets?'

'Well,' said Michael, 'the lady over there keeps tearing them up.'

Michael hadn't been with me long when he decided to take an HGV (a heavy goods vehicle) test. My mate Fred was his instructor, and when he came in for his usual short back and sides, he told me Michael was literally driving him nuts.

'First of all, I told him to let the clutch out,' said Fred. 'So he opened the car door. After that I gave him another instruction and we ended up in a village pond!'

'How come?' I asked.

'It was my fault,' said Fred. 'I told him to dip his headlights. I'm quitting before he drives over a cliff to test the air brakes!'

Poor Michael was always getting into scrapes. After being involved in an accident on his motorbike, he was asked by the police what gear he was in at the time.

'A crash helmet, leather boots, a bomber jacket and jeans,' he replied.

Then there was the day Michael found two corn plasters, so he went out and bought himself a tight pair of shoes.

One morning I came in to find a plaster on one of the mirrors.

'Here, Mike,' I said. 'What's all this?'

'Well, Maurice,' he said. 'I had this terrible boil on my back, and I had to look in the mirror to see just where it was – but I got it in the right place in the end.'

Mike's father was a butcher back home and one day, Mike told me, he was watching his father make sausages. The butcher put an ox into the machine, and sausages came out the other end.

The boy said to his father, 'Maybe one day they'll invent a machine that you can put sausages in and out will come an ox.'

'Invent one?' said the butcher. 'Your mother's got one already.'

'Mum says would you thin my hair out – it's too fat!'

20

But I couldn't believe it, one day, when Michael, only my assistant, remember, turned up for work at the barber's in a Rolls-Royce.

'What's with the Rolls, Michael?' I said. 'Won the pools?'

'Well,' said Michael. 'You know I live next door to Henley's the car people? They're always very good to me – I mean, they let me use the phone, they give me change for the gas and everything. I couldn't be a pig, could I? I had to buy something.'

I suppose the Rolls is why Michael got mugged coming home from work (though I'd made him take it back the next day, of course). Anyway, he was set upon by two hefty men, who obviously thought he was worth a mint. He fought like a tiger for ten minutes, but eventually they subdued him and pinned him to the ground. But after searching him, they only found 10p.

'Fancy you fighting and getting done over like that for a measly ten pence,' the muggers said to him.

'Aha,' came the reply. 'But I thought you were after the fifty quid in my socks.'

But the last time I saw Michael it was on the telly programme, *Mastermind*, when Magnus Magnusson asked him to define the meaning of the word *hereditary*.

'That's easy,' he said. 'It means that if my mother and father can't have children, I can't either.'

2
Every Tom, Dick and Hairy

(Some very funny customers)

Mannie, an old friend as well as a customer, was married to Sadie—a lovely woman, but perhaps tact was never her strong point . . .

One day, Sadie met Mrs Goldberg, who she hadn't seen for some time, while out shopping. But as Mrs Goldberg was off to Bournemouth for a fortnight's holiday, Sadie agreed to visit her on her return.

But when Sadie turned up on the appointed day, the doorbell was answered by Mr Goldberg, who told her that his wife had died that very morning. Very upset, Sadie nevertheless asked to see her friend. Mr Goldberg took her into the front room to see his wife lying in her coffin.

'It's hard to believe she's dead,' said Sadie. 'She looks so well!'

'She should do,' said Mr G. 'She's just had two weeks' holiday in Bournemouth.'

Mannie and Sadie went to an art exhibition, and were standing in front of The Birth of Christ.

Sadie: What a beautiful painting that is, Mannie. What a wonderful piece of workmanship!

Mannie: Very true, my darling, very true. But I can't help notice there's something very Jewish about that painting.

Sadie: Jewish? What do you mean – it's the birth of Christ! How can it be Jewish?

Mannie: Well, take a look – notice how poor they are – it breaks my heart they should be so poor. They are so poor that the boy is born in a barn surrounded by animals – but they could still afford for Rembrandt to come and paint the picture!

One day as Mannie was waiting for a shave, I noticed he was reading the newspaper.

'What's new then, Mannie,' I asked. 'World peace broken out yet?'

'Huh,' he replied. 'It says here that scientists have found a substitute for oil in camel dung. Great, eh – the only trouble is that the bloody Arabs have got all the camels.'

'Okay, Ali, fill her up!'

Mannie, a very proud father, sent his youngest son to Europe to study the violin. A few years later the boy returned, and his father hired the Albert Hall for his first concert. He told the family that if the boy was a success, he would book the Dorchester for a celebration party after the performance. The big night arrived – all the family had front row seats – and the boy was terrible. First of all his strings broke, then the violin went out of tune, he lost his place twice, and his sense of rhythm was non-existent. The audience was bored to tears. Realizing the night was a dreadful flop, Mannie rushed over to the Dorchester to cancel the dinner. When he got there he discovered three of his relatives sitting at the top table stuffing their faces.

'What the hell are you doing?' yelled Mannie. 'I told you I was only having a party if the boy's playing was a success!'

'Well,' said his second cousin. 'We liked it.'

When his oldest son told him that he was going to become a Christian, Mannie was inconsolable – his family had all pinned hopes on the boy becoming a rabbi. Desolate, he went into the synagogue, lifted up his head and wept. He was amazed to hear a voice, as he was the only one there.

'What is it, my son, what ails you?'

It was God!

'Lord,' said Mannie. 'I am so ashamed. My only son has renounced the Jewish faith and become a Christian!'

'Really?' said God. 'You too?'

Every morning the vicar of St Katherine's watched Mannie as he passed his church, and was puzzled to see, every morning, that he crossed himself. After several weeks of this, the vicar decided to tackle the Jew.

Mannie was as puzzled as the vicar. 'I don't know what you mean, Reverend,' he said. 'Every morning I come out of my house, and I say, Mannie, you've got your watch, you've got your wallet, and thank heaven your flies aren't undone.'

After being robbed during the night, Mannie's father, an elderly Jewish gentleman whose knowledge of the English language was limited, sent for the police. When they arrived they asked him to explain what happened.

'Vell,' he said, 'my wife she wakes me up in da mittle of da night and she say I theenk there's a buglar in da houze. So I jumpt outa bed and I get me ma gahn –'

'A gun?' says the detective. 'Do you have a licence for that gun, sir?'

'Since when do we havta haf a licence for a dressing gahn?'

At the reading of old Mr Abraham Rosen's will.

'Being of sound mind, I spent every penny before I died.'

Someone else I remember was an ex-assistant of mine who never had any luck – when he left me he went to work in a factory – but people don't change.

In the factory a raffle was held every week, and there was this one poor chap who never seemed to win anything. Week after week, his friends would win small to large amounts of money, but he never won a thing. After a while, his mates felt sorry for him, so they got together and decided to rig that week's raffle by putting his name on every ticket.

'Let him pull it out himself,' said his best friend, 'then he won't think it's been fixed!'

The chap was duly brought forward and told to pull out the winning ticket from the numbers in the hat. Closing his eyes, he drew out a slip and looked at it.

'Well?' asked his friend expectantly. 'Who's got it?'

'Burtons,' replied the chap. 'Six and seven-eighths.'

Harry Evans, a garage owner and regular of mine, was disturbed in the middle of the night by some noises in his kitchen, and crept downstairs to find a strange man standing in the middle of the room, holding a torch.

'What are you after?' said Harry.

'I'm looking for money,' said the man.

'Oh,' said Harry. 'Hold on a minute.'

He went to a drawer, opened it, and took out a torch.

'Right,' he said. 'Let's both look.'

Harry and Jim were waiting for a trim in the shop. They'd chatted for a while, when Jim said to Harry, 'You know, Harry, you're a fine friend. I'm surprised at you. We've been talking for half an hour and you haven't even asked me how I'm getting on yet.'

'Sorry, Jim,' said Harry. 'How are you getting on?'

'Huh,' said Jim. 'Don't ask.'

Meanwhile Jim and Harry's wives were also having a natter under the dryer.

'Where did you go for your holiday, Mary?' asked June.

'We went to the South of France. What about you?'

'We went for a trip around the world,' said June. 'It was all right, but next year we're going somewhere different.'

Harry, on a trip to Manchester, rang up Jim in London.

'Jim,' he said, 'could you lend me five hundred quid?'

'Harry,' yelled Jim, 'I can't hear you. Would you mind repeating that?'

'I SAID, WOULD YOU LEND ME FIVE HUNDRED QUID?'

'I still can't hear you, mate. There must be a fault on the line.'

'No,' interrupted the operator. 'There's no fault. I can hear both of you clearly.'

'In that case,' said Jim, '*you* lend him the five hundred quid.'

Jim and Harry were walking down the road when Harry noticed a pay packet lying in the middle of the pavement. Picking it up, he discovered a hundred pounds in it and a wage slip.

'What a bloody liberty!' said Harry.

'Some liberty,' said Jim. 'You find a hundred quid just sitting in the middle of the road, waiting for you to pick it up. Where's the liberty?'

'Yeah, I know,' said Harry. 'But look how much tax they've stopped!'

Oh yes, I know some funny customers all right . . .

Bert: How are you, mate?

George: Oh, all right, but these bills are a real pain. I've got so many I don't know which to pay first.

Bert: You ought to do what I do – I put 'em all in a hat, pick out one, and then that's the one I pay.

George: But what about all the others?

Bert: Any trouble from them, and I tell 'em – next time you don't go in the hat!

I used to suffer with a severe stammer, and my sympathies go out to those who still have trouble over their words, like my friend Tim . . .

A motorist asked him for instructions to get to the Elephant & Castle.

'You g-g-g-go to the t-t-t-urn-turn-urning on the l-l-l-eft up the Whi-Whi-Whi-te-tech-ch-ch-apel Road,' he began, 'past Aldgate Station, turn left and go up the M-M-M-M-Min-Min-neries where you t-t-t-t-t-turn right over to Tow-ww-w-w-wer Bridge and that will b-b-b-b-b-b-b-b-b-b-b-b-b-b-ring you up to the Bricklay-lay-ay-ayers Arms. T-turn r-r-r-right into the New Kent Road and that w-w-w-w-ill b-b-b-b-b-bring you up to the Elephant and C-c-c-c-c-castle.'

'Thank you very much,' said the motorist.

'Oh, y-y-yeah? I h-h-hope you get a bl-bl-bloody f-f-flat tyre.'

'Well that's nice,' said the driver. 'I only asked you the way.'

'Yes,' said poor Tim, 'but why out of all the b-b-b-b-leeding p-p-p-people you could have asked did it have to b-b-be m-me!'

Mind you – it's not always a disadvantage . . . Tim walked into his local betting office one day and went up to the counter.

'I've-I've-I've b-b-b-b-backed-backed-backed my win-win-w-win . . .'

'Sorry, Tim,' said the man behind the counter, 'but I'm busy and I can't deal with you now. If you've backed a winner, here's a fiver and you can collect the rest later, all right?'

Tim went outside with his fiver.

'S-s-strewth, what a generous bloke,' he managed to tell his mate. 'I was t-trying to t-tell him that I've b-b-backed my window-cleaning truck into his car and he g-g-gave me five quid!'

On Victoria station a man with a stammer addressed a second man waiting for a train: 'C-c-c-could you t-t-tell me what p-p-platform I g-g-g-go t-t-t-to f-f-f-for B-B-B-B-Brighton?'

The second man ignored him. But a third man standing nearby said, 'Platform 15, old boy.'

The first man thanked him and walked off. The third man said to the second man, 'Why didn't *you* tell him which platform?'

Tim replied, 'Y-y-y-you w-w-wouldn't w-w-want m-m-m-me to get a b-bloody n-n-nose w-w-would y-you?'

On Friday afternoons, OAPs were always half price, and Albert and Cissie were regulars. I overheard this conversation in the shop some time ago.

Albert: You know, Cissie, I don't think I'd like to fly in one of them aeroplanes – it gives me the heebie-jeebies just thinking about it.

Cissie: Don't be silly, Albert. They're as safe as anything. I mean, did you hear about that terrible train accident the other day? Three hundred and eighty-seven people killed!

Albert: Good lord! How come so many people were killed in a train?

Cissie: A plane fell on it.

Harry's dad was a tough old customer. No one would forget his passing in a hurry! Sid Evans was on his deathbed and his three sons, Harry, Jack and Joe, were sitting around him.

'He's sinking fast,' whispered Harry. 'We'll have to organize the funeral. We'll need three cars and a hearse.'

'What do we need three cars for?' asked Jack.

'One for us, one for relatives, and one for friends.'

'Nah,' says Jack. 'We never see his friends unless they want something. Two cars are enough and a hearse for dad.'

'What do we need two cars for?' said Joe. 'We never see the relatives either unless they want to borrow money. One car's enough and a hearse for dad.'

At this point the old man reached up and tugged Harry's sleeve.

'What is it, dad?' asked Harry.

'I'll go by bus,' he said.

Joe Evans had made himself a pot over the years, and his wife Minnie lacked for nothing. Her motto was 'never accept a fur unless it's in mink condition'. One day she even advertised for a butler.

After a week of unsatisfactory applicants for the post, a man turned up on Minnie's doorstep. He had no arms and legs.

Minnie asked him what she could do for him.

'I've come for the job,' he replied.

'But you're no good to me,' said Minnie. 'You've got no arms or legs.'

'Didn't I ring the bell?'

But despite her wealth, Minnie could never stand boasters.

One summer she and Joe were invited to a big society affair at Westminster, where a great many socialites and celebrities were expected to attend. Minnie had the misfortune to get button-holed by a particularly unpleasant MP's wife who would not stop going on about her vast fortune in precious stones and jewellery. First she explained how many she had, then where she kept them, then the history of each item, until poor Minnie's head was swimming. The wretched woman then went on to tell Minnie how she cleaned them.

'The diamonds I clean in gin for a real sparkle, but the rubies seem to come up better if I soak them in Amontillado sherry – of course, I wouldn't think of cleaning my priceless emeralds in anything but Napoleon brandy. The amusing thing, I find, is that the sapphires – which I think I mentioned are worth as much as the rubies and diamonds almost together – come up best after immersing them in nothing more extraordinary than a basin of pasteurized milk!'

'How amazing,' yawned Minnie, 'That you should clean them at all. When mine get dirty, I just throw them away.'

Minnie was always a sucker for charity. One day she donated a large sum of money for the construction of an indoor swimming pool at a local mental home. On the completion of the pool she was present at the opening ceremony and saw the inmates lining up on the top board and jumping off one by one with whoops of delight.

'Aren't they enjoying themselves!' Minnie remarked to the principal.

'They certainly are,' he replied. 'And just wait till we put the water in!'

Of course, Joe did start to put on airs after a while . . .

A Rolls-Royce pulled up outside an expensive Mayfair hotel, and the commissionaire on duty saw the chauffeur get out, immaculately dressed in a black uniform with gold braiding and a peaked cap. Inside were a couple dressed in furs with gold and diamond jewellery. The chauffeur picked up the man and carried him up the steps to the entrance of the hotel.

'Can't he walk?' asked the commissionaire.

'He doesn't have to,' said the chauffeur.

Joe was a shrewd businessman, and he never let up, even when he had made it. One day Joe went to the money-lenders and asked for a loan.

'Well, sir,' said the money-lender. 'You can borrow ten pounds, or five pounds.'

'I only want to borrow a fiver,' Joe told him.

The money-lender asked him for his address, and then if he had any collateral.

'Well,' said Joe, 'here's the keys to my Rolls-Royce. That should be all right, shouldn't it?'

The money-lender quickly agreed and lent Joe the five pounds.

Two weeks later Joe returned, looking bronzed and fit, to return the money with one pound interest on top. He handed the money over willingly, and as he was about to leave the shop with his keys, the money-lender called him back.

'Excuse me for being curious, sir,' he said, 'but surely a man of your means must have been in peculiar circumstances to need to borrow five pounds from a money-lender?'

'Of course I didn't need the fiver,' said Joe. 'But you tell me where else you can park a Rolls-Royce for a fortnight in London for a quid!'

Joe was quite a celebrity really – even went on TV, where they asked how he had come about his fortune.

'One day,' he said, 'I was broke and I borrowed a penny from a stranger to use the loo. When I got there, though, I found the bog door open, so I kept the penny and used it later in a pub fruit machine and won the jackpot. I used the jackpot money to bet on a horse, which came in at two hundred to one. I used my winnings to play in a card game and I won five thousand pounds. I bet with this money at a casino and made a hundred thousand. I put this money into stocks and shares, which made my my first million. From that day I have never looked back. My only regret is that I can't shake the hand of that man.'

'The one who lent you the penny?'

'No, the one who left the bog door open.'

But he had a heart of gold, Joe . . . a self-made millionaire, he was driving past his old street in his Rolls when he saw an old couple coming out of the Post Office and decided to do his good deed of the year.

'James,' he said to his chauffeur. 'Call that elderly couple over here and tell them I want a word with them, will you?'

When the couple arrived, Joe told them that he was a million-aire and that he would very much like them to be his guests on the holiday of a lifetime, all expenses paid. 'I want you two to go home, pack your bags and be back here at ten o'clock tomorrow morning,' he ordered, 'and I will get James to drive you down to Bournemouth.'

The next day, the couple were whisked off by the millionaire to the Plaza Hotel, where they were booked into a plush double suite with all mod. cons, colour TV, room service, etc. Joe made a point of telling the hotel manager to give them anything they wanted, and the very best of everything. Before he left, he shook them both by the hand and gave them each two hundred pounds.

'Enjoy yourselves,' he said, 'and I'll be back with James in a fortnight to pick you up in the Rolls.'

The fortnight went very quickly, and the millionaire returned as promised to pick up the two sun-tanned pensioners.

'Well,' said the millionaire. 'How was it?'

'Marvellous! You're a wonderful, generous and warm-hearted man, sir, and I can't thank you enough,' said the old boy. 'We did everything – ate like kings, saw plenty of shows, went to the cinema, had lovely weather – in fact there was only one thing that bothered me a bit.'

'Oh yes? What was that?'

'Who the hell's the old lady?'

Probably one of my funniest customers was Luigi, the little Italian fellow who ran a pizza place down the road. I'll never forget his account to me of his holiday in Malta . . .

'One day ima gonna Malta to bigga hotel,' he said. 'Ina morning I go down to eat breakfast. I tella waitress I wanna two pissis toast. She brings me only one piss. I tella her I wanna two piss. She say go to the toilet. I say you no understand, I wanna two piss onna my plate. She say you better no piss onna plate, you sonna ma bitch. I don't even know the lady and she call me sonna ma bitch! I tella you, Maurice, I no understand theesa forrinners! Anyhows, later I go to eat at the bigga restaurant. The waitress brings me a spoon and knife but no fock. I tella her I wanna fock. She tell me everyone wanna fock. I tell her you no understand. I wanna fock on the table. She say you better not fock on the table, you sonna ma bitch. So I go back to my room inna hotel and there is no shits onna my bed. Call the manager and tella him I wanna shit. He tell me to go to toilet. I say you no understand. I wanna shit on my bed. He say you better not shit onna bed, you sonna ma bitch.

'I go to the checkout and the man at the desk say: "Peace on you". I say piss on you too, you sonna ma bitch. I tell you, Maurice, I gonna back to Italy next year!'

Pat and Spike were inseparable comrades – but they were always getting into trouble, basically because they had about half a brain cell between them. One night the two of them were trying to get home to Hackney after a drunken evening in the West End. They came to a deserted bus garage.

'Go in and get a Number 38,' Pat said to Spike, 'and we'll drive ourselves home.'

Five minutes later Spike emerged from the garage. 'They've only got Number 19s in there, Pat.'

'That's all right. We'll take two of them instead,' said Pat. 'Now I'll go down to the bus stop and you can pick me up there.'

So Spike went inside, started a bus, but drove right past Pat at the stop. Pat had to run after the bus all the way to the next one.

'Why didn't you pull up at the last stop, you idiot?' he said to Spike.

'Well,' said Spike primly, 'you didn't put your hand out, did you?'

Pat and Spike were given two donkeys. But Pat was worried that he wouldn't be able to tell which donkey was his, so he cut off a bit of the donkey's ear. Unfortunately, unknown to Pat, Spike had similar worries and had done the same. So Pat clipped a little off the donkey's mane. But Spike had already done the same. Finally, Pat docked the donkey's tail, but the next morning when he saw Spike, he realized that Spike had also cut his donkey's tail.

'Look,' said Pat, 'this is daft. We'll straighten this out once and for all. You put a collar on your brown one, and I'll give me white one a chain.'

Pat and Spike went on a camping holiday. One night they camped in a field just beyond the road. In the morning they got up at dawn, packed their tent, and walked out of the field on to the road. Just then, a car came tearing around a bend in the road. Seeing them, the driver swerved off the road and into a field, his car coming to a halt on the exact spot where Pat and Spike had spent the night.

'Bloody hell,' said Spike, 'it's lucky we got up early, otherwise we'd have been run over in our sleep.'

Pat and Spike both decided to buy a car. Together, they went to their local dealer, and each purchased a Volkswagon Beetle. They drove off in convoy, Spike following Pat. At a red traffic light, Pat stalled his car and was unable to start it again. Finally he got out of the car and went to the front, lifting up the hood.

Spike saw him staring into it in amazement. He got out of his own car and went over to his friend.

'No wonder the bloody car won't start,' said Pat. 'It hasn't got any engine.'

'Not to worry,' said Spike. 'I've got a spare one in my boot.'

Pat and Spike won £40,000 each on the pools. They went to the West End to receive their cheques. After the ceremony, they were walking back to their suite in the Ritz and realized that they were both peckish.

'Would you fancy a pie, Spike?' said Patrick.

'That I would,' replied Spike.

So they stopped at the very first fish and chip shop they came to and bought a couple of steak and kidney pies.

'This is on me,' said Pat, paying for them both.

Carrying on down the road they passed a plush car showroom, exhibiting an impressive display of Rolls-Royces, Bentleys and Mercedes.

'Well now,' said Spike. 'How do you fancy a Rolls, Patrick?'

'That would be grand,' replied Pat through a mouthful of steak and kidney pie.

So they went inside and selected two immaculate Rolls-Royces, one gold, one silver, and each fitted out with every extra imaginable. On being presented with the bill, Pat went for his cheque book, but was stopped by an indignant Spike, who made him put it back in his pocket.

'Come on now, Patrick. I'll get these. After all, didn't you pay for the pies?'

3
Keep Your Hair On!
(Some prickly customers)

I knew an actor who had an incredibly inflated ego. One day he called at the shop in a pensive mood.

'Maurice,' he said. 'Why do you think so many people take an instant dislike to me?'

'Saves time,' I said.

The same chap was called to the stand to testify in a minor breach of contract case. When asked to identify himself, he said: 'I am the world's greatest actor!'

Later, after the court had adjourned, one of his friends tackled him about the boast.

'Don't you think that was a bit thick, old man,' he said. 'The world's greatest actor? I mean –'

'Normally,' replied his pompous pal, 'I would shun all sorts of self-praise, but this time they had me under oath. I *had* to tell the truth!'

In a restaurant a man ordered chopped liver. On tasting it, he called over the waiter and said, 'I've got two complaints. First, this chopped liver tastes like manure.'

'I'm very sorry, sir,' the waiter said. 'And what's the second one.'

'You give such small portions!'

After being served his first course in a very high class restaurant, a diner called the waiter over.

Diner: I'm afraid I simply cannot eat this soup.

Waiter: But, sir! The soup is our speciality. No one, but no one has ever complained about it before!

Diner: I can't help that – I just can't eat it!

The head waiter, hearing the commotion, rushed over to the table.

Head Waiter: Really, sir, I cannot believe that you cannot eat our soup. Do you realize that many of the Crown heads of Europe come here just to eat that soup?

Diner: Oh yeah? And did you give *them* a spoon?

Karl Blatvsky was what you might call a nitpicker – I can't remember many people missing him when he returned to his native land . . . he was walking down the West End one day when he passed the Empire, Leicester Square.

'Plees,' he asked the commissionaire, 'vot is zee name of zis sinnima?'

'This cinema,' replied the commissionaire, 'is the EMPIRE, LEICESTER SQUARE, the most luxurious cinema in Western Europe!'

'Reely,' said the tourist. 'And ow much iz eet to go in?'

'Two pounds, three pounds and five pounds,' came the reply.

Karl mused for a moment, then said, 'And when I walk to my five pound seat in zis fine sinnima – do I walk on ze nice carpet for my feet?'

'Oh yes, sir,' replied the commissionaire. 'Our carpets are made by the most famous manufacturers in the world.'

'Hmm,' said the tourist. 'And when I am seeting in my five pound seat and I look around – am I seeing the nice murals on ze walls?'

'Oh yes, sir,' replied the commissionaire. 'This cinema was built by the greatest architect in London and the interior is famous for its luxury.'

'And when I am seeting in my five pound seat are there the lovely young ladies coming around with ze ice-cream and ze cigarettes and ze confectionery?'

'We have the best catering staff in London, sir,' the commissionaire replied.

'I see,' said the tourist. 'And thees film which you are showing – what eez that?'

'Ah yes, sir, a most popular item, sir. "Doctor Jekyll and Mr Hyde", sir. Highly recommended.'

'Mm,' said Blatvsky. 'This doctor. He is a specialist?'

For some people food is more than a quick sandwich and a pint of beer . . .

A man went into the confectionery department at Fortnum & Mason and approached an assistant.

'I understand that you specialize in making wedding and party cakes,' he said.

'That's correct, sir,' she told him.

'In that case,' he said, 'I'd like an eleven tiered walnut sponge cake, covered with vanilla and strawberry icing with a bell that rings on the top.'

'Certainly, sir. Would you mind repeating that order?'

'I'd like an eleven-tiered walnut sponge cake with vanilla and strawberry icing and a bell that rings on top.'

The assistant wrote down the details. 'That will be thirty-five pounds sir. We'll have it ready by Tuesday.'

On Tuesday the man returned to the shop to find the most magnificent cake waiting. Except that it only had ten tiers.

'I asked for eleven tiers,' he said, with tears in his eyes.

'I'm so sorry, sir,' said the assistant. 'If you come back tomorrow I'm sure it will have been put right for you.'

The next day he returned to find that the extra tier had been added to the cake. But the bell on top didn't ring. He was beside himself. The assistant apologized again and asked him to come back in half an hour.

When he returned he found that the bell rang beautifully and he was finally satisfied.

'Shall I have it wrapped and delivered to you?' asked the assistant.

'Oh no need to go to all that trouble,' said the man blissfully. 'I'll eat it here.'

One day a man walked into the barber's shop and saw Ron, an awkward customer if ever there was one, waiting with a dog sitting beside him.

'Does your dog bite?' he asked Ron.

'No,' said Ron.

He stroked the dog, and the dog bit him.

'I thought you said your dog didn't bite.'

'That's not my dog.'

George was talking to Ron. 'I saw a good film last night – "Moby Dick".'

'I don't like sex films,' said Ron.

'It wasn't about sex. It was about whales.'

'I can't stand the bloody Welsh either.'

Ron got on a 149 bus at Stamford Hill and asked the coloured conductress for a ticket to Selfridges.

'Man,' she says, 'we don' go to Selfridges.'

'Of course you do,' he replied.

'I tell you we don' go to Selfridges.'

But Ron doggedly continued to insist that she was wrong, so infuriating the conductress that she stopped the bus and asked the Cockney driver if the bus went to Selfridges.

'No,' he said.

She turned back to the passenger. 'You should be satisfied now, honey,' she said. 'You've got it in black and white.'

A Jewish man went into Levinsons and asked for an ice-cream.

'I'm sorry, sir,' said the proprietor. 'We don't serve Jews.'

'But you're a Jew yourself,' said the customer. 'This is disgraceful!'

'Have you tasted our ice-cream?'

Harry met Reuben in a street in Golders Green, and Reuben invited Harry to visit him.

'When you come,' he said, 'press the lift button with your left elbow, open the doors with your right elbow, take the lift to the third floor, open the doors with your left elbow, press the door button with your right elbow –'

'Hold on,' said Harry. 'What's all this left elbow, right elbow stuff?'

'Well,' said Reuben, 'you won't be coming empty-handed, will you?'

An attendant at a swimming baths told his friend that he had been given the sack for urinating in the pool.

'Everybody does that,' said the friend.

'What – from the top board?'

One day we were all amazed to see a very famous actor walk through the door. He asked for a haircut and I tried to engage him in light conversation, but it was soon pretty obvious that he thought rather too much of himself to talk to the likes of me. As he left to go, he placed fifty pence in my hand as a tip. I gave it back to him, saying, next time I'd go and watch him perform.

'I'll have you know,' the pompous fellow said, 'that *I* do not give any fifty pence performances!'

'All right,' I said, showing him the door, 'then I'll come and see you twice!'

I knew two customers – Cohen and McTavish – who were both very mean. They never gave any tips and were always haggling over the price of a haircut. I wondered which of the two was the meanest, and decided to find out. So I invited them both out for a lavish four-course meal at a smart restaurant. At the end of the meal I pretended to have forgotten my wallet.

'I'll pay,' piped up McTavish, to my surprise.

I went home chuckling, amazed at McTavish's generosity – but a couple of days later I saw a headline in the newspaper: JEWISH VENTRILOQUIST FOUND STRANGLED.

An American farmer from Texas was being shown around a typical British farm. At the end of the tour he said 'It's a quaint little farm. But, d'you know, back home I can get into my car at seven o'clock and drive and drive and drive all around my farm and I don't get back home until four o'clock.'

'Oh I know,' said the British farmer. 'I had a car just like that once.'

One day a man walked into our local pub and asked the barman for a pint of beer and two pickled onions. He took the pickled onions, put them behind his ears and drank the beer before walking out. The next day, exactly the same thing happened: the man ordered a pint of beer and two pickled onions, put the onions behind his ears, then drank the pint and left. This happened for six days in a row. The barman was intrigued by this, and when the man came in on the seventh day and asked for a pint and two pickled onions, he said, 'I'm sorry, sir, we only have gherkins.'

'In that case,' said the man, 'they'll have to do.'

The barman fetched him his pint and the two gherkins, which the man duly placed behind each ear. He drank his pint and started to walk out.

'Excuse me, sir,' said the barman. 'But every day you've come in here, ordered a pint of beer and two pickled onions, put the onions behind each ear, drank your pint and gone. Now today you've drunk your pint and put two *gherkins* behind your ears. It's ridiculous – why on earth do you do it?'

'Well,' said the man, 'you haven't got any pickled onions, have you?'

Old Cissie was a game old girl, but she couldn't half complain! One morning she caught the postman as he was on his round.

'Hoy! You!' she yelled. 'What's been happening to my post? I sent off for some medicine over a week back, and nothing's arrived.'

'A weak back?' said the postman. 'That's funny, I've got a weak back. What do you take for it?'

'I'm not interested in your back trouble young man! I want to make a complaint!'

'Oh, well, in that case, you have to fill in a form and state the nature of your complaint.'

'If you must know, it's gas in the stomach.'

I know Bill and Ben were flowerpot men, but I knew a Bill and Ben who were just plain potty . . .

Bill and Ben, two inmates of a lunatic asylum, were bored and decided to play shops.

'Four bananas, please,' said Ben.

'Wait your turn,' said Bill. 'Get in the back of the queue.'

Ben waited a while, then said, 'Four apples, please.'

'I told you before,' Bill said. 'If you don't wait your turn I'll smack you in the nose.'

'Four oranges then,' said Ben.

Bill smacked him straight on the nose, and sent Ben sprawling across the room. At this point a warden walked in and saw Ben lying in a crumpled heap on the floor.

'Who hit him?' he asked Bill.

'How should I know,' said Bill. 'I had a shop full of customers.'

Bill and Ben both escaped from the asylum.

'Let's split up,' said Bill, 'and I'll meet you by the town hall at seven o'clock.'

'OK,' Ben agreed.

At seven o'clock Bill was waiting outside the town hall when Ben drove up in a big car.

'Where the hell did you get that?' asked Bill.

'Well,' said Ben, 'I met a beautiful girl who picked me up in her car. She drove me into the country, took off all her clothes and told me I could have anything I wanted.'

'Cor – anything?' said Bill.

'Yeah,' said Ben. 'So I took the car.'

'You did right,' agreed Bill. 'Her clothes wouldn't have fitted you.'

Bill got on a train, intending to travel to Crewe. The ticket inspector looked at his ticket and told him that the train wasn't stopping at Crewe.

'But I have to get off at Crewe,' said Bill, 'otherwise I'll miss my connection. Here, give this fiver to the driver and ask him to slow down as we're passing through Crewe so that I can jump off. And here's another fiver for yourself.'

The inspector went off and returned five minutes later.

'The driver's agreed to slow down as we pass through Crewe so that you can jump off,' he said 'but don't forget to start running the moment you jump off, otherwise you'll fall over and break something.'

Bill remembered this advice, and when the train slowed down at Crewe he jumped off and started running down the platform alongside the train. As the last carriage passed him, the guard grabbed him by the lapel and yanked him back on the train.

'Lucky I saw you, mate,' he said. 'You nearly missed it.'

4
A Head for Business

(Well, you've got toupée the rent)

It's a pity that Mr Begin is no longer president of Israel – he and Mr Reagan used to get on so well, they were always happy to do business together . . .

Reagan: You know Mr Begin, you have no idea how tough it is, being president of a country with over two and a half million citizens.

Begin: Believe me, Mr Reagan, it's no tougher than being a citizen in a country with two and a half million presidents.

Reagan: Menachim, I'm very impressed with your troops. They're extremely tough in the line of fire. Any chance of letting me have a few battalions on an exchange basis?

Begin: Ronnie, they're yours. All I want in return is a couple of your generals.

Reagan: Great. Which two d'ya want?

Begin: General Electric and General Motors.

An Englishman, a Jew and an Arab were sitting in a railway carriage when a fly flew in through the window. It landed on the Englishman's nose, but he flicked it on to the nose of the Jew, who in turn flicked it on to the nose of the Arab, who promptly ate it.

A few minutes later a second fly flew into the carriage, again landing on the Englishman's nose. He flicked it on to the Jew's nose. The Jew immediately grabbed it and said, 'Anyone want to buy a fly?'

On being released from prison after serving five long years, a man found a shoe-repair ticket in his jacket pocket. After presenting it to the cobbler he was told, 'They'll be ready on Friday.'

Chaim and Aaron were good boys, who were both in the Israeli Army. But they never stopped moaning about it . . .

Chaim: You know, Aaron, I blame Moses for all our troubles.
Aaron: Moses? But how can you blame our great leader Moses?
Chaim: You're joking. If he'd only turned left instead of right when he crossed the Red Sea, the *Arabs* would have got all the sand, and *we'd* have got the oil.

My brother fell into an upholstery machine. But now he's fully recovered.

My old friend Mannie went to the White House to see President Reagan some years ago. On the desk were three telephones: a blue one, a white one and a red one.

'Why three telephones?' asked Mannie.

'On the red one I talk to Begin,' Reagan replied. 'I ask him if he needs any planes, ships or tanks. On the blue one I ring up Moscow, etc. And on the white one I talk to God.'

'I'd like to talk to God,' said the Jew.

'It'll cost you a hundred dollars,' said Reagan. 'To talk to God, it's worth it.'

Mannie agreed. He dialled God, talked for a while, then left.

After America he flew to Israel and met Begin, who also had three phones on his desk. It was a similar arrangement.

'I see you have three telephones,' said Mannie. 'Why so many?'

'Well,' said Begin. 'On the red telephone I talk to Reagan in case I need any guns or planes or anything, on the blue phone I talk to Sadat, and on the white phone I talk to God.'

'I sure would like to talk to God,' said Mannie.

'It'll cost you ten pence,' said Begin.

'Ten pence!' cried the Jew. 'But Reagan charged me a hundred dollars!'

'Of course,' said Begin. 'But this is a *local* call.'

'*Divine inspiration don't come cheap – but I'm thinking of moving the White House nearer to Heaven to save on the calls!*'

Customer to waiter in a grand hotel: Do you serve crabs here?
Waiter: We serve anyone, madam.

Harry Rosen had a thriving dry goods business, but one day, two rivals moved in on either side of him. The rival on the left put up a big sign saying WE HAVE MADE A BIG MISTAKE – MUST VACATE! HIGHEST VALUE CLOTHING AT LOWEST PRICES!!!

Not to be outdone, the rival on the right put up a sign saying BANKRUPTCY SALE – CLOSING DOWN! EVERYTHING AT LEAST HALF PRICE!!!

Harry Rosen put up a sign: MAIN ENTRANCE TO BIG SALE!!!!

Charlie: Tom, why have you converted to the Jewish faith? I thought you were an atheist.

Tom: I was, but you try going all year without a holiday.

Two Israeli soldiers, Chaim and Aaron, were discussing the hardship that their war with the Egyptians had made them suffer.

Chaim: You know, what we ought to do is declare war on the United States. They will beat us, and then like all the other countries they defeat, they'll send in tons of food, billions of dollars in aid, give us all houses and factories and send all our kids to high school . . .

Aaron: You're joking, Chaim. With our luck, we'd win.

One thing about working in England is the wonderful sense of comradeship you get commuting into town every day with the same people . . .

Four men in a train who were used to commuting together each day were held up one morning when the train stopped in a tunnel. There was a very uncomfortable silence.

Deciding to break the ice, one gent who was normally used to hiding behind *The Times* lowered his paper and said, 'I used to be a brigadier, I'm married, I have four sons and they're all solicitors.'

The *Telegraph* reader sitting by the window, not to be outdone, lowered his paper and said proudly, 'That's remarkable. *I* used to be a brigadier too. I'm married with four sons who're all doctors!'

The *Guardian* reader sitting opposite remarked, 'That's incredible – because I'm an ex-brigadier as well, I'm married and I have four sons who're all barristers.'

At this they all looked at the last member of the group, who peeked over his *Daily Mirror*, placed on his lap and sighed. 'I was a sergeant,' he said. 'I'm not married, and my four sons are all brigadiers.'

At a building site manned by Irish labourers, a monkey kept throwing bricks at all the workers. Finally the foreman turned to one of his men and said, 'Paddy, get that monkey and take him to the zoo, otherwise he's going to hurt someone.'

Paddy took the monkey away and was gone for over two hours. When he finally returned, the monkey was still with him.

'Paddy,' said the foreman, 'I thought I told you to take that monkey to the zoo.'

'I did, boss,' said Paddy. 'But he didn't like it much, so I took him to the cinema.'

A firm of Irish contractors were hired to build a hotel on the top of Everest. Halfway up they ran out of scaffolding, so the foreman said, 'Let's go down now. Sure we can do the rest to-morrow.'

An Irish parachute training corps were being lectured.

'When you fall out of the aircraft,' said the instructor, 'wait until you're six feet from the ground, then pull the cord to open the parachute.'

'What if the parachute doesn't open, sir?' asked a raw recruit.

'Come on, sonnie,' said the instructor sarcastically. 'You can jump six feet can't you?'

My daft ex-assistant Michael had difficulty finding a job after he left hairdressing. They would keep on giving him tests . . .

There was one job he applied for where they asked him to take an intelligence test consisting of three questions. The first question was, 'What has four fingers and a thumb and is made out of wool or leather?'

Michael thought for a while, then shook his head. 'I don't know.'

'A glove,' said the examiner.

'Oh yeah,' said Michael. 'I knew that, really.'

'Second question,' said the examiner. 'What has eight fingers, two thumbs and is made out of wool or leather?'

Again Michael pondered before saying, 'Er, I don't know.'

'Two gloves,' said the examiner. 'Last question. Who lives in the Vatican, wears a mitred hat and is loved by millions of people all over the world?'

Michael thought very hard and then grinned. 'Three gloves?'

Michael applied for another job, and this time the personnel manager gave him an English test.

'Now, Michael,' he said, 'I want you to give me a sentence with the word WELLINGTONS in it.'

'I went into the shop and bought a pair of WELLINGTONS,' replied Michael.

'Very good,' said the Manager. 'Now give me a sentence with the word SHIRT in it.'

'I went into the shop and bought a pair of WELLINGTONS and a SHIRT,' said Mike.

'Very good,' said the Manager. 'Now how about a sentence with the word FASCINATE in it?'

'I went into the shop,' said Michael, 'and bought a pair of WELLINGTONS, a SHIRT and a duffle coat with nine buttons on it – but I could only FASCINATE of 'em!'

Michael eventually managed to get a job as a cab-driver, but he gave it up after a week because he didn't like people talking behind his back.

Tom: I hear your store was burgled yesterday, Jim.
Jim: That's right, mate. Thank God it wasn't today.
Tom: Why's that?
Jim: Yesterday everything was marked down twenty per cent.

Of course, the main thing in a partnership is trust . . .

Jack and Harry, partners in their own business, went to the pub for an after-work drink.

'Jack!' said Harry. 'I forgot to lock the safe!'

'That's all right,' said Jack. 'We're both here, aren't we?'

Thomas to friend: You know, Jim, I'm really in debt. I'm on the verge of bankruptcy. I haven't a penny. The worst thing is, I haven't the faintest idea where I'm going to look for the money!

Jim (relieved): Thank God for that. For a minute there I thought you were going to borrow it from me!

A jewellery shop was held up. During the investigation . . .

Jeweller: You won't believe this, officer, but the shop was held up by an elephant!

Inspector: What sort of elephant? African or Indian?

Jeweller: How should I know? It had a stocking over its head.

Mannie Goldberg had a very successful little business in the middle of a busy street and was dismayed when a large supermarket was due to open directly opposite his shop. The supermarket advertised a host of bargains, and when Mr Goldberg saw butter advertised at 40p a pound, he put a sign in his own window saying 35p a pound.

Furious, the supermarket manager came to see him. 'How can you sell butter at thirty-five pence a pound?' he asked. 'It costs more than that wholesale.'

'What should I care?' said Mannie. 'I don't even sell butter!'

My friend Jacques was a fastidious sort of bloke. I wasn't at all surprised when I learnt he'd landed a job. But I was a bit taken aback when he told me how he got the sack . . .

He'd got the job, as a waiter at the Ritz, after telling the manager how very conscious he was of hygiene. On his first day the manager noticed a fork in his top pocket, and asked him what it was for.

'You see, I never touch ze food with my fingers,' the Frenchman explained. 'I am always using ze fork.'

The manager was very impressed, and went away. Some time later he noticed a piece of string sticking out from the Frenchman's trousers.

'Jacques,' he said. 'Please explain.'

'Well when I go to ze toilet,' Jacques said haughtily, 'I pull it out with ze string so that never I am touching it with ze hands.'

'You're a credit to the restaurant,' said the manager. 'But one thing bothers me. How do you get it back in?'

'With ze fork!'

Jobs being so hard to come by these days, it's incredible what some people will consider doing for a living . . .

A circus advertised for a lion tamer and received two replies: one from a man, the other from a very attractive young girl. The girl was the first applicant. She stepped calmly into the ring, walked into the lion's cage and waited for the lion to come towards her. As he did so, growling and roaring, she undid the top of her sequined costume, and let it fall to the floor. The lion stopped in his tracks, then started towards her again, this time licking his lips and snarling softly. As he closed in, the girl undid the lower half of her costume and stood there completely naked. The lion stopped, then walked straight up to her and started licking her face, then her arms, then her legs, then all over.

'Well,' said the circus manager. 'D'you think you could do that?'

'Not half,' said the man. 'Just get that lion out of the cage and I'll prove it!'

Of course, some folks are never off duty . . .

Two judges collided in their cars on a country road. Neither was hurt, but they decided to set up court and fine one another for careless driving.

'How do you plead?' the first judge asked the second.

'Guilty, m'lud.'

'I'll fine you five pounds,' said the judge. 'And don't do it again!'

Now it was the second judge's turn.

'How do you plead?' he asked.

'Guilty, m'lud.'

'I'll fine you twenty-five pounds.'

'What!' said the first judge. 'I only fined you a fiver!'

'Yes, I know,' said the second, 'but this is the second case of careless driving we've had today and I've raised the fine to prevent an epidemic.'

If you're looking for bargains, it's amazing what you can pick up in the market . . .

George was selling strawberries off a barrow in the suburbs. When he asked a pretty young girl if she wanted to buy some, she told him to go round the back of the market. When he got there, to his surprise she was standing in a doorway without a stitch of clothing. Disgusted, he turned away.

'What on earth's up with you?' she said.

'Listen,' said George. 'Today my wife ran away with my best friend, I've just lost three thousand quid on the stock market, my horse came in last and my son forgot to post a pools coupon that would've won me thirteen-and-a-half grand. And now you want to screw me out of my strawberries?!'

Sadie was always looking for bargains, but somehow she never seemed to look in the right places . . .

Sadie entered a greengrocer's and asked for a pound of apples and a pound of pears.

'Thank you, madam,' said the greengrocer. 'That'll be one pound fifty.'

'One pound fifty? That's rather expensive, isn't it?'

'Well, sir, this is a high quality fruiterer's,' came the reply. 'We sell only the best.'

'In that case here's two pounds and you'd better keep the change – I trod on a grape as I came in.'

A fruiterer at a stall was calling out, 'Ten pence a pound eating apples! Ten pence a pound eating apples!'

Sadie thought that this was a good bargain, so she bought three pounds. But on inspecting the apples she turned back to the fruiterer.

'These aren't eating apples,' she said. 'They're cookers.'

'Lady,' said the man. 'Why quibble? After all, what are you going to do after you've cooked them?'

Sadie went to another stall, where the man was calling, 'Five oranges for ten pence! Five oranges for ten pence!'

'I'll take five,' she said, handing him the ten pence.

Walking away, she saw that she only had three oranges in the bag. She returned to the stall. 'I paid you ten pence and you've only given me three oranges,' she said.

'Yes, you see when I weighed 'em, two was bad, so I threw 'em away.'

I don't know. Even in a depression tailors always seem to do all right. Maybe it's their ability to cut their cloth to suit our needs . . .

Mr Jones went to Mr Goldberg the tailor to get fitted for a suit.

'What's your name?' asked Mr Goldberg, taking out a ledger. 'Where do you work, what are your politics, what's your wife's name, how many children do you have –'

'Wait a minute,' said Jones. 'What's all this about? I only want to be fitted for a suit, I don't want to join the Masons or anything!'

'I'm a perfectionist,' Mr Goldberg replied. 'I send all these details to a sheep farm in Australia where it gets processed. A sheep is then picked out to suit your particular personality, they cut the wool off the sheep, dye the wool, make it into mohair, cut the cloth, send it to me, I make two or three fittings, and deliver it –'

'Hold on – I need it by Friday.'

' – and deliver it by Friday!'

58

A boy of eighteen started work in a menswear shop. On his first day, the boss left him alone to serve the customers, but unknown to the boy, watched him from a back room. On the first sale, the boy sold a shirt for £6 – he put £4 in the till, and the remaining £2 in his pocket. The next customer needed some ties. The boy sold him two at £2 each – he put £2 in the till and £2 in his trouser pocket. On the next sale, the customer bought a cardigan for £9 – and this time the boy put the whole £9 in his pocket and nothing at all in the till. Seeing all this, the boss came into the shop.

'What's the matter, Billy?' he asked the boy. 'Aren't we partners any more?'

Mr Cohen was measuring Mr Jones for a suit when he remarked on how well Mr Jones was looking.

'You look wonderful,' he said. 'Have you been on holiday?'

'I certainly have, Mr Cohen. I went on a cruise on the *QE2*. It was wonderful – I met a gorgeous girl with red hair and green eyes and a perfect figure. She gave me a marvellous time.'

'My God!' said Cohen. 'My daughter works on the *QE2*! A girl with red hair, green eyes and a marvellous figure – it could have been her! It could have been my daughter!'

'Well,' said Mr Jones, 'if it was, it's the first thing you've ever made that fitted.'

I went to the tailor's to have a suit made.
Tailor: Do you want a belt in the back?
Me: Do you want a kick in the teeth?

A short-sighted toastmaster had a new pair of ceremonial trousers made by Mr Rosenberg, an East End tailor. A few days later he was officiating at a reception for the Chamber of Commerce which was attended by Mr and Mrs Rosenberg. While waiting at the door to be announced by the toastmaster, Mr Rosenberg listened to the introductions.

'Brigadier and Mrs Cameron,' said the toastmaster. 'Colonel and Mrs Anstruther.'

Mr Rosenberg was next.

'Your name, sir?' enquired the toastmaster.

'You know me,' said Mr Rosenberg. 'I made your trousers.'

'Major and Mrs Trousers,' announced the toastmaster.

A man had a new suit made at a high-class tailor's, but when he got home he found that the trousers were too tight in the crotch.

He took them back to the tailor's, but found only a lady assistant on duty.

'Can I help you?' she said.

Embarrassed, he said, 'Well, I've had this suit made here, but I'm afraid there's something wrong with the trousers.'

'I see,' said the woman. 'What exactly is wrong with them?'

'Well, you know Centrepoint at the end of Oxford Street?'

'Yes.'

'You know the ballroom inside?'

'There's no ballroom inside!'

'That's right – and that's what's wrong with these trousers.'

Marty Rosenstein was a manufacturer of coats, but business had been getting so bad that he was finding it difficult to get off to sleep at night.

'You ought to do what I do,' I told him. 'Try counting sheep!'

Marty promised to give it a try, but the next morning when I saw him on the train, he looked worse than ever.

'Marty!' I said. 'You look terrible! What happened? Didn't you count sheep like I told you?'

'Count sheep!' retorted Marty. 'I should say I counted sheep. I counted up to fifty thousand sheep, and when I had done that, I couldn't help but notice all that lovely fleece going to waste, so I sheared them. After that, I spun the wool, washed, dyed and dried it, wove it into a lovely bit of worsted, cut out fifty thousand suits in top quality style – then I decided that they needed fur collars, so I started counting rabbits. When I'd counted fifty thousand rabbits, I skinned them, washed, dyed and dried the fur, cut out a pattern and stitched them on to the coats. They looked terrific! I was just about to fall asleep, when I thought of a terrible problem that kept me awake the rest of the night.'

'After all that! What problem!' I asked.

'Where the hell do you buy fifty thousand silk linings wholesale at four o'clock in the morning?'

When it's all too much, there's always the open road . . .

A rep. broke down on the M1, out of petrol. He flagged down an Irishman who asked what the trouble was.

'I'm out of petrol,' said the motorist.

'That's all right mate,' said the Irishman. 'Get in behind me, I've got a tankful!'

A rep. driving up the M1 had a crash. He ran down the road to a garage.

'Quick,' he said, 'I've just had a crash and I need a pick-up truck.'

The mechanic began to take down the details.

'What sort of car is it?' he asked.

'A Ford Concertina,' the man replied.

'Don't you mean a Ford Cortina?'

'You haven't seen my car!'

Housewife to salesman: I suppose you've had a lot of doors
    slammed in your face.
Salesman: No madam. I'm afraid I've always looked like this.

A rep. phoned the AA: 'Please, you've got to help me. I've locked my keys in the car.'

'We'll be there as soon as possible, sir.'

'Please hurry – it's raining cats and dogs and I've left the sun roof open.'

Everyone says schooldays are the happiest days of your life – well maybe not everyone . . .

Charlie was eating his breakfast with a very sulky face.

'Charlie, will you hurry up!' said his mother. 'You're going to be late for school again!'

'I don't want to go to school today,' said Charlie.

'Come on,' said his mother. 'You've got to go.'

'I hate school.'

'Why?'

'I don't like the teachers, I hate all the boys, and all the boys hate me.'

'Charlie,' said his mother. 'You've got to go. You're the headmaster – who else is going to take prayers?'

5
Letting Your Hair Down

(Time off for bad behaviour)

Many of my customers follow the horses and a barber should always be ready with a word of advice . . .

Barber: How's the horses been treating you lately, George?

George: Terrible – can't seem to get a winner these days. I think the racing's slowing off.

Barber: No it isn't. I'm still getting results all right. But then, every day before I place a bet, I go to church and pray. And the next day, the Good Lord answers my prayers.

George, very impressed, decided to try the same thing. Two weeks later, he returned for his trim.

Barber: Well, how did it go?

George: Terrible – I didn't have one winner.

Barber: I can't believe it – which church did you go to?

George: The big Catholic one just down the road.

Barber: That explains it, you idiot – that one's for the hurdle racing.

Well-to-do gambler to friend: 'I always come back from the casino with a small fortune.'

'How come?' asked his friend.

'I go in there with a bigger one.'

Pat O'Reilly won £50,000 on the football pools, and decided to treat himself to the best watch he could find. After scouting around the West End he went to the most exclusive jeweller in the area, who showed him a beautiful watch at £5000, which, he assured Pat, was absolutely accurate and would not lose one second. That night, Pat settled down to watch TV and the 'Nine O'Clock News' came on. Looking proudly down at his new watch, he was horrified to see that it said a quarter to eleven!

'Bridget!' he yelled to his wife, 'how many times have I told you not to mess around with this telly?'

The manager of an Irish football team was given the sack during the middle of a hard winter when his team was beaten three times on the Pools Panel.

After spending three months at Gamblers Anonymous, Tom said to the leader of the group, 'I want to thank you for everything you've done for me. And I'll bet you a tenner I'll never gamble again!'

Sid and Harry were gin rummy addicts.

'Look Harry,' said Sid. 'I know you've been fooling around with my wife, but I still love her. Let's settle this in a civilized way – I'll play you a game of gin rummy, and the winner takes the missus.'

'OK, mate,' agreed Harry. 'But just to make it interesting, how about playing a penny a point?'

Returning home in the early hours of the morning after winning £2000 at a casino, a man crept into bed next to his sleeping wife and slipped the money under his pillow. When he woke in the morning and put his hand under the pillow he was horrified to find that it was not there. His face went white.

'What's the matter, dear?' said his wife. 'You look terrible.'

'Not surprising,' said her husband. 'I don't feel too grand.'

A barber's Irish friend was playing bingo with him.

'Thirty-two, sixty-one, forty-seven,' the Irishman said to him.

'Look at your own card,' said the barber.

'That's all right,' said the Irishman, 'mine's full up.'

Due to an unfortunate trick of nature, Nigel was born with three testicles. As he grew to manhood, after many years of discomfort and embarrassment, he finally accustomed himself to the fact, and thought no more about it. One day, he went to the races, having discovered the joys of gambling, and had a very bad day with the horses, losing a substantial amount of money. At the end of the racing, Nigel approached the bookie who had practically cleaned him out and asked him if he would be interested in a private bet.

'Well,' said the bookie. 'What sort of thing did you have in mind?'

'What odds would you give me,' said Nigel, 'that we've got five testicles between us?'

A bit taken aback, but still game, the bookie replied that he'd give Nigel a hundred to one.

'You mean you'll lay down one hundred pounds to my one?' said Nigel.

'That's right, lad,' said the bookie.

'You're on.'

'Good,' said the bookie, taking his trousers down. 'Well, here's my one. Where's your four?'

A Jew and a Scotsman went fishing together and agreed that whoever caught a fish would be given £1 by the other.

The Jew pulled in a haddock and the Scot gave him a pound. A little later, the Scot pulled in a plaice, but the Jew only gave him 25p.

'What's the idea?' said the Scot.

'We pay quarter the odds a place,' replied the Jew.

One weekend, Harry invited his friend George down to the exclusive country club of which he was a member for a game of squash. George was delighted, and the two had an extremely enjoyable and competitive game, after which Harry suggested that they both go to the bar for a drink. George agreed, but said that he really needed a shower first. Unfortunately, he misunderstood Harry's directions, and, after getting hopelessly lost, ended up, quite unknowingly, in the ladies' shower-room. After an invigorating shower, he put the towel over his head and walked into the steam-room, where he lay down, exhausted, with the towel over his face, and closed his eyes for a few minutes. Suddenly he heard female voices.

'Well, he's not my husband,' said a woman's voice.

'No,' said a second woman, after a pause. 'He's not my husband either.'

'Huh!' said a third woman, after an even longer pause. '*He's* not even a member of the club!'

A famous golfer was having a drink in his club when a man bumped into him, causing him to spill his drink.

'Look where you're going, you fool!' he shouted, whereupon the man apologized and shuffled away.

'I think you were out of order there,' said the golfer's friend. 'You know, that man was blind.'

Filled with remorse, the golfer went after the blind man.

'I'm so sorry,' he said. 'I had no idea of your disability.'

'That's all right,' said the blind man, 'you weren't to know. By the way , aren't you that famous golfer?'

'As a matter of fact I am.'

'I'd love to play a famous man like yourself at golf.'

'Wouldn't that be rather difficult for you?'

'Oh, you'd be surprised. I have a marvellous caddie who comes with me on the fairway. He lines me up, hands me the right club, and I hit the ball. If I'm on the green, he stands behind the hole and whistles so I get an idea of how far away it is. I do quite well.'

The golfer was impressed. 'As I was so rude to you,' he said, 'I'd be happy to give you a game.'

'Marvellous. And how about a little side bet?'

'A side bet? Oh no, I couldn't.'

'Come on – how about a hundred quid a hole?'

'A hundred pounds a hole! Are you absolutely sure about this?'
'I'm sure. As long as you let me pick the time and place.'
'All right, you're on.'
'We'll meet at the first tee here tomorrow.'
'Fine – and when?'
'At midnight.'

A retired barber was persuaded by his family to join the local golf club. The first day he visited the club, he walked into the bar and asked for a double Scotch. Seeing as it was his first day, he decided to treat the other members, too.

'Drinks all round,' he asked the barman.

'That's all right, sir,' the barman replied, when the barber went for his wallet.

'Drinks are on the house.'

Feeling pretty pleased about this, the barber then asked where he could get golf balls. The barman told him and, finishing his drink, the barber sauntered off to the stores. He was amazed when the attendant charged him £20 for each ball. Later on, the barber's son came to pick him up in his car.

'How was it, Dad?'

'Well, son,' said the old man, 'I tell you this. They don't catch you by the drinks!'

Four archbishops arranged to play doubles at golf. But on the morning of the game, only three of them turned up.

'What are we going to do?' they asked one another.

At this point, a fiery chariot descended from the clouds, and a bearded man in flowing white robes stepped out.

'I'll make up a foursome,' he told them.

The three archbishops agreed. At the first hole, a 500-yarder, the bearded man asked for a putter.

'Who does he think he is?' said one of the archbishops. 'God?'

'He *is* God,' said another. 'He *thinks* he's Arnold Palmer.'

Joe Evans drove his Rolls into the car park at his local golf club and got out. A young boy immediately ran up to him.

'Are you going to play golf, mister?' asked the boy.

'That's right,' said Joe.

'Can I clean your car for you while you're away?'

'All right. Do a good job and I'll give you a fiver.'

Two hours later, Joe returned to find his Rolls gleaming.

'Excellent work,' he said to the boy. As he reached into his pocket to give the lad his money, two golf tees fell out of his wallet.

'What are they?' asked the boy.

'They're to put your balls on,' Joe explained.

'Blimey,' said the boy. 'Rolls-Royce think of everything!'

A barber decided to take up golf as a pastime, so he hired a profesional instructor who took him out to the local golf course. At the first tee the professional said, 'I want you to hit this ball four-hundred-and-twenty-five yards on to the green.'

The barber hit the ball hard, and it landed inches from the hole.

'Now what do I do?' he asked.

'You hit it into the hole,' said the professional.

'Why didn't you say that the first time?'

A golf fanatic was marooned for a whole year on a desert island. Things were pretty dull, as he was all alone, but one morning, as he was having his usual coconut breakfast, to his astonishment he saw a beautiful blonde swimming towards him from the ocean. Rubbing his eyes, he rushed down the beach to greet her. After he had helped her ashore, she asked him how long he had been there. On finding out that it was a whole year, she looked sympathetic, and asked him if he would like a cigarette. Disbelievingly, the marooned man watched as she took a packet of Rothman's out of her bikini top, a lighter from a belt round her waist and sexily lit him up a cigarette.

'After a whole year, I should think you could do with a drink, too,' she breathed huskily at him.

'Not half,' said the stranded golfer, amazed as she took out a full bottle of Scotch from a hip flask strapped to her thigh, and duly poured a generous measure into his coconut shell.

'Well now,' she whispered provocatively. 'How would you like to play around?'

'I don't believe it,' he cried with delight. 'Don't tell me you've brought a set of golf clubs as well!'

A married couple were very keen golfers, and one night the wife asked her husband: 'George, if I was to die, would you marry again?'

'I daresay I would.'

'Would you let your new wife live in this house of ours?'

'Why not? It's a lovely house.'

'Would you let her sleep in our bed?'

'I don't see why not. It's very comfortable.'

'What? And would you let her use my golf clubs?'

'Certainly not.'

'Oh, George, why not?'

'She's left-handed.'

Heimie was playing golf. The ball sliced, hitting a car driver on the head. The car driver swerved his car across the road, slammed into a coachload of tourists that slid into the central reservation, hit an oil tanker that in turn went straight under a train. There was a dreadful crash, an explosion, and fifty people were killed. The caddie looked at Heimie, and said, 'Did you see that? You just hit that driver on the head with the ball, he swerved across the road, slammed into that coachload of tourists, the coach slid into the central reservation, hit that oil tanker, and the tanker blew up under the train killing at least fifty people!'

'Oh dear,' said Heimie. 'What on earth can I do?'

'Well,' said the caddie. 'If you change your grip to something like this, you can go *round* the ball.'

A rabbi was playing golf on the sabbath. On the trickiest hole on the green, a hole which he had never been able to sink under 4, he gave the ball an almighty whack, so that it flew straight as an arrow into the hole for a perfect hole in one. With tears in his eyes, the rabbi looked up to heaven. 'Who can I tell?' he cried.

Of course, the easiest way to let your hair down is to have a couple of drinks – but there's always them as will go too far . . .

One night, far from home, George got extremely drunk in a pub. He made such a nuisance of himself, in fact, that the landlord was forced to throw him out. Hardly the worse for wear, and unrepentant, George fell in through the saloon door and asked for another pint.

'Oh no, my lad,' said the landlord. 'You're going out!'

And he picked George up by the scruff of the neck and threw him out of the saloon door and back into the street. Undeterred, George picked himself up and staggered into the pub through the snug door. 'A pint of bitter, may mahn!' he said, 'and make it snappy!'

'YOU!!' bellowed the landlord, picking George up by the back seat of his trousers and hauling him out through the snug door. 'Get out of here and stay out!'

George calmly followed the kerb round to the front door of the pub and entered on his hands and knees. Coming up against a very large pair of brogue shoes and a pair of muscley legs, he found himself staring straight into the nostrils of the landlord.

'A pint of bitter, dear sir,' mumbled George, as he was trans-ported bodily through the air.

'Get out of my pub!' yelled the furious landlord, hauling George out on to the street like a sack of coals and dumping him in the gutter. 'You bloody pest! AND STAY OUT!!'

'Tell me,' said George. 'You own *all* the pubs round here?'

George went gratefully back to his local, the Coach and Horses, to find that they had installed a new barmaid, a pretty young girl who was easily flumoxed.

'You know, it's six months since I've been in here,' said George nostalgically.

'Look,' she replied. 'This is my first night – I'm serving as fast as I can!'

You just never know who you're going to meet in a pub . . .

In an Italian bar, Mario was having a Dubonnet, when he observed a man across the bar from him wearing a wellington boot on his head. Deciding it must be a touch of the sun, he had another drink and looked again. The man was still there. Mario, a little shaken, took another drink and looked back over the bar to find the man still wearing a wellington boot on his head, staring across the bar back at Mario. Realizing he had been spotted, Mario swigged back another drink and approached the man with the boot on his head.

'Excuse me, *signor*,' he began. 'I could not help but notice you are wearing this wellington boot upon your head. Forgive me, but I cannot help but ask why on earth you should be doing such a thing?'

'Aha,' said the man with the wellington boot on his head. 'I always wear a wellington boot on my head on Tuesdays!'

'But *signor*,' replied Mario, 'today is Thursday!'

'Oh my god,' said the man. 'I must look bloody ridiculous!'

A man walked into a bar, ordered two pints of Guinness, put one on the floor and drank the other down in one. He ordered another two pints, picked the now empty glass from the floor, replaced it with the new one, and drank his own. The barman, understandably intrigued, looked over the end of the bar and saw a tiny man, about three inches high, supping up the pint on the floor.

'Good grief!' said the barman. 'Who on earth or what on earth is that?'

'You just be careful, mate,' said the tall man. 'That's my mate John and he don't take no lip from nobody. We've been all the way round the world together in the army. From Saigon to

Bangkok, Korea, Aden, Hong Kong, Africa to um . . . John, where was it you called that witchdoctor a schmuck?'

Harry and Archie were firm friends for years, and as Harry rose in his career he made sure that Archie was not left out of all the extra socializing and high society events that came with his job. Unfortunately, Archie had a terrible knack of disgracing himself after having too much to drink, and though Harry still regarded him as a friend, he had to tell Archie that enough being enough, he couldn't invite him to any more high class parties, as he was giving him a bad name. Months went by, and one night, Harry bumped into Archie as he was on his way to a particularly important function. When Archie knew where his friend was off to, he begged to be taken along, swearing that he was a reformed character.

Harry reluctantly allowed himself to be persuaded, and the two set off together. The evening was splendid, with excellent food and wine, and after the meal, the guests were all invited into the drawing room to participate in games. They played a game called the guessing game, in which a lady would put her hand into her handbag, and ask the other guests to guess what she was holding in her hand. After a few rounds of this, and several brandies, Archie announced that it was his turn. Putting his hand in his pocket, he loudly urged the party to guess what he was holding in his hand.

'Is it a bunch of keys?' asked the hostess.

'No,' replied Archie

'Is it your wallet?' guessed his host.

'Wrong,' said Archie.

'I know, it's a lighter!' said another lady guest.

'No,' said Archie laughing. 'It's me balls!'

Poor Harry hid in the corner as the dinner host ordered Archie to be removed forcibly from the gathering. Thrown out in the street in the rain with his hat and coat, Archie quickly sobered up and realized what a terrible scene he'd just caused, and decided that for Harry's sake he had to go back and apologize. He rang the bell and came face to face with the butler who had just thrown him out.

After much pleading, the butler reluctantly brought the host out and despite a pretty frosty reception, Archie stammered out many heartfelt apologies. The host, much impressed with his sincerity, accepted the apology and shook Archie's hand.

'James,' he said. 'Take this man's hat and coat. We all make mistakes, my boy,' he said generously, 'and I could see you'd had a drop too much to drink, so come on back in, and we'll say no more about it.'

Archie rejoined the party, and after a couple of hours more conviviality, the other guests accepted him as if nothing had happened. As the party continued into the small hours, and the cocktails and cigars had circulated plentifully, one of the lady guests suggested that they play the guessing game. Archie volunteered to start.

'Is it a packet of cigarettes?' asked the host.

'No,' replied Archie.

'Is it a bunch of keys?' asked the hostess.

'No,' replied Archie.

'I know, it's your wallet,' said a guest.

'No – fetch my hat and coat, James, it's me balls again!'

But if you spend the night on the booze, there's always the chance of a fight breaking out . . .

In the pub Pat got into a fight with a much bigger man, and suffered a prolonged beating until at last he was lying on the floor.

'Had enough now?' said the big man.

'Enough?' said Pat. 'I don't know. This is only my first fight.'

Pat, drunk, said to Spike, 'Did you just pour your beer in my lap?'

Spike shook his head sadly. 'I'm afraid not, Pat my boy,' he said. 'What you have there is an inside job.'

And then there's the problem of how you're going to get home . . .

A man walked out of a pub near closing time on a Saturday

night, reeling from side to side. He staggered through the crowded car park, got into his car and drove off.

The police car parked nearby immediately screamed off in pursuit, sirens blaring, and made him pull over. They breathalysed him, but to the policemen's surprise the test was negative.

'Would you mind coming down to the station for a blood test?' asked one of the policemen.

'No,' said the man, hiccuping loudly, 'I wouldn't mind at all.'

They took him down to the police station and gave him the blood test. This also proved negative.

'I just don't understand it,' said one of the policemen. 'I'd have sworn you were drunk.'

'Drunk?' said the man. 'Who are you calling drunk? I'm just the decoy.'

A man entered a crowded bar.

'Drinks all round,' he said to the barman, 'and have one yourself.'

Everybody's glass was filled.

'That'll be eighteen pounds fifty,' said the barman, supping his drink.

'I haven't got any money,' said the man.'

At that, the barman leapt over the bar, gave the man a good thrashing and bundled him out of the bar.

A few weeks passed. The man returned to the bar and, unrecognized by the barman, ordered drinks all round.

As the barman was filling up everyone's glasses he said, 'Does that include me, too, sir.'

'Not likely,' said the man. 'Give you a drink and you go bloody mad.'

In a collision between two cars, one driver was knocked out and the other escaped without a scratch. The unhurt man rushed over to the unconscious driver and gave him a drop of whisky – and then another, and another, and another.

When the police turned up they wanted to know who was responsible for the accident.

'Smell him,' said the unhurt driver.

A drunk staggered up to a policeman.

Drunk: Ekscuse me, Ossifer. Can you direct me to the nearest Alko-holliks Anominnos?

Policeman: Want to join up, eh?

Drunk: No, no. I want to resign.

Perhaps the best thing is to get away from it all . . .

After spending a holiday in England, an American was waiting for the flight home when an Englishman asked him what he'd thought of England.

'It was great,' he said, 'but I didn't like your weather.'

'Why not?'

'Because you get spring, summer, autumn and winter.'

'They get that everywhere,' said the Englishman.

'All in one afternoon?' came the reply.

A beach is a great place to get an all-over tan . . .

An elderly man was taking the sun on the beach one day, when a lady walked by and, pointing to his crotch, said 'Your shop's open!'

'Clear off!' said the old man, 'and leave me in peace. What's the matter with you!'

'Well,' said the woman, 'your shop's open!'

'Leave me alone!' said the old man. 'Get out of it and let me sleep!'

'If you don't believe me,' she said, 'take a look!'

At this, the old man looked down and realized that his flies were well and truly undone.

'Oh dear,' said the old man. 'You were right, the shop was open. Tell me, miss, was the manager in or out?'

Some, of course, are forced to take their holidays at Her Majesty's convenience . . .

An Englishman, an Irishman and a Scot were sentenced to ten years in prison. Discussing ways to pass their time, the Scotsman took out a pack of cards from his pocket. 'We can play solitaire till the cows come home,' he said.

The Englishman said that he was very fond of chess, and that he had a travelling set that would keep him occupied.

The Irishman smiled, and said that he had something better than either game. '*I've* got a packet of Tampax!' he said happily.

His friends looked puzzled. 'What on earth can you do with those?' they asked.

'Well,' said Paddy. 'It says here on the packet you can go riding, swimming, skiing, play tennis . . .'

While others . . .

George was walking down the street when suddenly he was taken short. Across the road was a public convenience. As he went inside, he saw the attendant sitting outside in a deckchair with his trousers rolled up to his knees, a handkerchief knotted over his head, and wearing a pair of sunglasses.

77

'What on earth are you doing?' asked George.

'I applied to the council for my summer holidays,' said the attendant, 'and they told me to take them at my own convenience.'

A man walking his dog on the beach one morning was amazed when suddenly his dog keeled over and died. Despite all attempts to revive him, the dog just lay there, dead as a doornail. A Jew was passing by, and asked the man what was the matter. On being told, he immediately bent down and gave the dog mouth to mouth resuscitation. The dog sprang to life as if by magic, and dashed into the sea, where he splashed about happily. The Jew rushed in after him, grabbed his lead and gave him back to his grateful owner.

'That was truly fantastic,' said the owner of the dog. 'You a vet?'

'Of course I'm a vet,' replied the Jew. 'In fact, I'm a bloody soaking!'

While travelling in Africa, Spike picked up a gorilla as a souvenir of his holiday – but even he was bright enough to realize that he would have trouble getting the animal through customs – so he slapped a piece of heavily buttered bread over each of the beast's ears and approached the customs desk as if he had nothing to declare. The customs official thought Spike looked pretty suspicious, so he turned all of his cases inside out before he was satisfied. Just before he let Spike go, he suddenly noticed the gorilla.

'Hello, hello,' said the official, 'and what's this when it's at home?'

'Now look here,' said Spike furiously, 'I don't mind you turning over my baggage, but what I choose to put in my sandwiches is my business!'

One day when they were on the beach, a little boy turned to his father and said very loudly, 'Dad! I want to piss!'

'You mustn't say that, son. I told you. When you want to go to the toilet, you've got to say "I want to whisper!"'

'All right, dad,' the little boy agreed, and every time he wanted to go to the toilet, he used the word 'whisper'. One day, when his auntie was taking him out shopping on the bus, the urge came upon him and he started jumping up and down, saying 'Auntie, I want to whisper, I want to whisper.'

'Calm down, dear,' she said firmly. 'That's quite all right. You come over here and whisper in my ear.'

A Scot, an Irishman and a Jew, on holiday in Africa, were driving across the desert when the car broke down, leaving them stranded.

'Well,' said the Jew, 'I'm going to take up the leather from the seats, so that when I'm desperately hungry, I'll have something to chew!'

'And I'm going to take out the radiator,' said the Scot. 'At least there's *some* water in it for when I'm desperately thirsty!'

'Righto,' said the Irishman. 'I'm going to take off one of the car doors. Then I can always wind down the window if it gets too hot.'

Of course, you can always go to a show . . .

Henry was dreadfully bullied by his overbearing wife.

'Get out there, you lazy bum, and do the shopping,' she yelled at him one Saturday. 'And don't come back till you've bought everything I want. Including a fresh chicken for Sunday!'

Poor Henry set off, and managed to buy everything except for the fresh chicken – the shops only seemed to stock frozen. Knowing he'd get a rocket if he went back home with the wrong thing, he asked everyone he could where to find a fresh bird.

'Well,' said a helpful butcher. 'Old Jones sells chickens straight from the farm, but it'd be a live one, mind.'

Well, thought Henry, *you can't get much fresher than that!* So off he set for the farm and bought himself a nice plump chicken. Feeling quite pleased with himself now for having got the shopping done so quickly, he happened to pass the cinema on the way home, which was showing one of his favourite James Bond films. Deciding that his wife would never know, he was about to buy a ticket when he suddenly remembered the chicken. *They'll never let me in with this*, he thought. But he really did want to see the film, so he finally hit upon the idea of hiding the bird down his trousers. Glad to be out of his wife's clutches for an hour or so, he happily paid his money and took a seat in the dark cinema. He soon got engrossed in the film, but felt a definite discomfort in his trousers. *Poor little devil*, he thought. *As it's so dark, no one will notice if I let his head out for a breath of fresh air!* So he undid his buttons, pulled the chicken's head through, and settled back to enjoy the film, totally unaware of the consternation of the two women sitting next to him. After a while, he heard,

'Here, Ena. The bloke next to me has, you know, he's got his, you know, he's got his *thing* out!'

'Don't worry, Hettie,' replied her friend, a common-sensical soul. 'Once you've seen one, you've seen them all!'

'Yeah, I know,' said Hettie. 'But this one's just eaten all my Smoky Bacon crisps!'

Two sailors spent the evening getting very drunk together and afterwards went to see a variety show. Halfway through the performance one of the sailors had to get up to go to the toilet. On asking directions from an usherette he was told, 'Turn first left, then first right, then first left again.'

The sailor, practically blind drunk, took three left turns by mistake and found himself in an empty space. He relieved himself there and returned to his seat. At the end of the show he turned to his friend and said, 'That was a really good show. I really enjoyed it.'

'You missed the best act,' said his mate. 'While you were out, a sailor came out on stage and pissed all over the band!'

A ventriloquist was sitting on a stool doing his act, his dummy on his lap. He made several offensive jokes at the expense of the Irish. After a while, a man in the audience stood up.

'Hey, you!' he shouted. 'I'm Irish, and I object to you making fun of me and my countrymen.'

'I'm sorry,' said the ventriloquist. 'I didn't mean to offend you.'

'I'm not talking to you,' said the Irishman. 'I'm talking to that cheeky little bugger on your lap.'

Many customers, though, like to entertain at home . . .

Two old school rivals met for the first time in many years.

'Well, Harry!' said George. 'Haven't seen you since you sung in the choir! What have you been doing with yourself?'

'So much has happened, George!' said Harry. 'Where can I start? Well, firstly, I'm married. I have three lovely children, and taking after us, they're all very interested in music. One son plays the drums, my daughter plays the flute, and the youngest son plays saxophone. Sometimes we get up a little musical band in the evenings with the wife on violin and myself playing the piano. You ought to come round one evening and we could give you a recital! How about you? Still interested in sports?'

'Yes,' replied George. 'I'm married too, you know, and the whole family is involved with the martial arts. I'm a black belt in Judo, my wife's a brown belt, the eldest son's learning Kung Fu and the youngest's a karate expert! Come round some night and we can kick your head in!'

An Englishman, an Irishman and a Scot wanted to go to the Olympic Games, but they had no money to buy tickets. Nevertheless, they arrived at the stadium determined to get in by pretending to be competitors. At the gate, the Englishman took off his plimsolls, hung them over his shoulder by the laces, and strolled past the guard, saying, 'Johnson, England, the eight hundred metres!' The guard let him through.

The Scot, winking at the Irishman, picked up an iron pole left over from some scaffolding, and hurried past the guard with, 'McTavish, Scotland, the javelin!' and was waved through.

The Irishman looked around desperately for something to get him past the gate, and finally returned with a roll of barbed wire. 'Murphy, Ireland,' he called cheerfully. 'Fencing!'

Jim joined a social club. On his first night, the secretary proceeded to show him around the club. After seeing the darts room, the TV room, the pool room, etc. he came upon a group of people sitting around a small stage. As Jim watched, a man got up from the audience and said quietly, 'Forty-three!' – at which the whole audience broke into laughter. Puzzled, Jim looked at the secretary for an explanation, but he, too, was in fits. Meanwhile, a woman had taken the man's place on the stage, and said into the microphone, 'Seventeen!' Again, the audience erupted with mirth.

'What . . . ?' asked Jim, but again the secretary was speechless, holding his sides and screaming with laughter. By this time, a third member of the audience had got up on the stage, and after pausing for a moment, whispered into the mike 'Fifty-nine!'

This time the audience really went berserk, hooting with laughter and screaming hysterically. The secretary was on the floor.

'I don't understand,' said Jim.

'Well,' said the secretary, wiping his eyes. 'Every month we issue a club jokebook, in which every joke is numbered – each member gets a copy, and they only have to say the number, and everyone in the club gets the joke.'

What a great idea, thought Jim. 'Where do I get my copy?'

The secretary gave Jim the little jokebook, which he took eagerly home to study. All week, Jim memorized the jokes and their numbers, ready for the next Saturday night. He was so excited that as soon as he entered the club, he made straight for the room with the little stage, where there were already a number of people calling out numbers.

Jim rushed on stage, picked up the mike, and screamed, 'Number three!' very loudly. There was a stony silence. A bit taken aback, Jim tried a better joke. 'Forty-four!' he said enthusiastically. Still no response. As his last resort, Jim tried the very funniest joke in the whole book. 'Seventy-two!' he said triumphantly.

But no reaction at all came from the audience, and Jim was forced to leave the stage without getting a single laugh.

'I don't believe it,' he told the secretary. 'Last week they were all going mad – and I know I got all the numbers dead right. I told them the best joke in the book, too, but they didn't laugh once!'

'Yes, I'm sorry,' said the secretary. 'It's the way you tell 'em!'

6
Hair Indoors

(Samson loved Delilah until she bald him out)

*The doctor told me not to take my worries to bed with me. I said,
'She'd be lonely sleeping on her own.'*

Do you remember how the old song goes . . . ?
    'Oh how we danced on the night we were wed
    We danced and we danced
    For the room had no bed.'

*My poor friend Willie was as henpecked as can be – I remember him
telling me about his honeymoon . . .*

'I got married the same day they bombed Pearl Harbor,' he
told me. 'A double catastrophe. When we got to the hotel – a
lonely place with hot and cold chamber maids – the wife
suggested we took single beds. "Single beds!" I said. "Don't be
silly. You'll get a terrible cold walking around in your bare feet."

'At 2.30 in the morning, the wife nudged me: "Turn that
wireless off, darling."

' "That's not the wireless," I told her, "that's the band in the
ballroom."

' "It's the wireless," she said.

' "No, it's the band in the ballroom."

' "It's the wireless!"

' "Look," I said, "I'll prove it."

'So I jumped out of bed, wearing only my shortie nightshirt,
and went downstairs. When I came back I said, "It was the band
in the ballroom."

'The wife instantly burst into tears.

'"What's wrong?" I asked. "What are you crying for?"

'"Well," she said, "tomorrow when we go down to breakfast they'll all point you out as the man who went into the ballroom in his nightshirt."

'"Don't be silly," I told her. "I didn't want them to recognize me so I threw it over my head."'

After 35 years of marriage, a barber took his wife back to the hotel where they spent their honeymoon. While unpacking, his wife remarked, 'Do you remember the first time we came here? You didn't even give me a chance to get my stockings off.'

'I certainly do, darling,' he replied. 'Now you've got time to knit a pair.'

Later the barber took his wife out to the zoo. She wanted to feed the monkeys, but was told that they were mating.

'Do you think they'll come out if I rattle my bag of nuts?' she asked her husband.

'Would you?' he replied.

At the next stop on their journey, the barber and his wife wanted to book a room in a hotel. Entering the reception area of a very grand-looking establishment, the barber asked the man on duty if he had any available rooms. After checking the reservations, the receptionist said, 'I'm sorry, sir. There's only the bridal suite.'

'What do I want with the bridal suite?' said the man. 'We've been married thirty-five years.'

'Well, sir,' came the icy reply. 'I can give you the ballroom but you don't have to dance.'

A very wealthy couple were making love on their honeymoon.

'Darling,' said the woman, 'do poor people do this?'

'Oh yes,' her husband replied. 'I believe so.'

'Hmm. Far too good for them, isn't it?'

An insurance salesman was trying to sell a young housewife a policy on her husband's life, but was not having much success in getting through to her. In the end, he tried another approach.

'Look at it this way, Mrs Brown,' he said. 'If your husband died tomorrow, what would you get?'

Mrs Brown thought for a moment and then said, 'Probably a budgerigar.'

On their thirtieth wedding anniversary, Sid and Muriel decided to holiday in Paris for a weekend. After an exhausting Friday and Saturday shopping, sightseeing and spending each night on the town, they were so tired that they slept in on the Sunday morning.

When Sid got the bill from the manager he was appalled. 'Four hundred francs for one night! It's ridiculous! It's extortionate! I won't pay it!'

'But *monsieur*,' said the manager. 'It is inclusive, the bed and the breakfast.'

'But we didn't have any breakfast,' said Sid.

'That is a shame, *monsieur*, but it was there if you wanted it.'

'OK,' said Sid. 'There you are.' And he handed over 200 francs to the manager.

'But, *monsieur*,' said the manager. 'The fee is *four* hundred francs, not two.'

'Well,' said Sid, 'all last night, you made love to my wife.'

The manager was horrified. 'It's not true, *monsieur*. I did not do such a thing!'

'Maybe not,' said Sid. 'But it was there if you had wanted it!'

George to Harry, comparing notes.

'My wife is so ugly,' said George, 'she got a job outside our chemist's, making people sick. In fact when she walks into the kitchen, the mice jump on the chairs and scream.'

'I know, mate,' said Harry. 'You don't have to tell me about women. I bought my mother-in-law a new armchair for Christmas, but the wife won't let me plug it in.'

At the dance hall a young man went up to a girl and asked her for a dance.

'I don't dance with kids,' she sneered.

'Oh I'm sorry,' he said. 'I didn't realize you were in that condition.'

I was always terrified of women when I was young. I'll never forget my first dance . . .

I walked up to a girl and asked her, 'Can I have this dance?'

'Of course,' she said, 'if you can find a partner.'

That's nice, I thought. But eventually I did find a partner – she was deformed – instead of having a bosom in front, it was round the back. She wasn't much to look at, but she was terrific fun to dance with!

Wife: You know sometimes I get the feeling that you're ashamed to go out with me.

Husband: Don't be silly, darling. Just wait till it's dark, and I'll take you for a walk.

Gas man collecting the money from the meter: How come there are so many foreign coins in here?

Sadie: Well, I don't really know, but I do a lot of continental cooking!

Mrs Brown was complaining to her next door neighbour.

'My Alf's so lazy he does nothing – just sits in front of the telly all day.'

'My Bert's just the same.'

'I bet he's not as lazy as my Alf. He hasn't even got the energy to switch on the set.'

Arthur took his secretary out for a dinner one night. Afterwards he ended up at her apartment and didn't leave until long after midnight. Going home in the early hours of the morning, he took a cue chalk out of his pocket and rubbed it all over the sleeves and elbows of his jacket.

'Where the hell have you been?' screamed his wife the minute he walked in the door.

'If you must know,' said Arthur, 'I took my secretary out for dinner, went back to her place afterwards and made mad passionate love to her for three hours.'

'You bloody liar,' said his wife, looking at his jacket. 'You've been out playing snooker with those lousy friends of yours again.'

I always wear the trousers in my house. Mind you, the wife always tells me which pair to wear!

In heaven, St Peter told all the men, 'I want all the men whose wives have dominated them to stand on my left, and all those who have not been dominated by their wives to stand on my right.'

Everyone moved to the left except for Arthur, a little man with glasses.

'What are you standing there for?' called out one of his friends.

'My wife told me to,' he said.

Two Jewish women met up for the first time in many years.

'Sadie,' said one. 'You're looking wonderful. What have you been up to?'

'Well,' said Sadie. 'I'm having an affair.'

'Really?' said her friend. 'Who's the caterer?'

Women like to bring out the animal in a man. Preferably a mink.

Sadie: Ach, Minnie, first love is so romantic!

Minnie: Ah yes. I'll never forget how I fell in love with my Bernie at second sight.

Sadie: Minnie, you schmeil, don't you mean first sight?

Minnie: Not at all. At first sight I had no idea he was a millionaire!

Sadie met her old friend Dolly while she was under the dryer one day.

'Dolly!' said Sadie, 'how well you're looking! And so smartly dressed! You look lovely. Is that a new locket you're wearing?'

'Yes,' replied Dolly. 'It's a remembrance locket.'

'Really? What's in it?'

'A lock of my husband's hair,'

'But, Dolly, I saw him this morning – your husband's still around!'

'Ach, yes, Sadie. But his hair isn't.'

Sadie: How's your daughter, Minnie? I hear she's married now.

Minnie: Sadie, that girl – she has married a prince! Every morning he lets her stay in bed till eleven o'clock. She never has to put her hands in cold water, and all afternoon all she has to do is mix herself cocktails!

Sadie: Minnie, that is wonderful. And what about your son Herbie?

Minnie: What can I tell you? That boy has broken my heart. You wouldn't believe the slut he's married. She stays in bed till eleven in the morning, never dreams of putting her hands in cold water, and she's such a lush she lies round all afternoon drinking cocktails!'

Just before dawn, the head of New York's top department store was woken by the telephone.

Woman: Oh, Mr Bloomingdale! I am so pleased with the hat I ordered from your store. I love it. It is simply fabulous!

Mr B: At four o' clock in the morning you are ringing just to tell me that?

Woman: Well, they've only just delivered it!

Sadie (sunbathing in Miami with her friend Minnie): Doesn't it make you feel small looking at the ocean, Minnie?

Minnie: You think that's big? And you're only looking at the top.

One interesting guy that came into the shop was a chap who told me that he'd been married three times, once to an Italian, then to a Frenchwoman, and was now married to a Jewess.

'My goodness,' I said. 'They must have been very different!'

'You're not kidding,' said my customer. 'When I made love to my Italian wife, she'd scream "Gino, Gino, you are fantastico –

the world's greatest lover! Kissa me! Kissa me!" And when I made love to my French wife she would cry, "Jean, Jean, – tu est formidable! More, chéri, more!" Now I'm married to Rachel, when we make love it's always, "Johnnie, how many more times do I have to tell you that ceiling needs painting?".'

George won £100 on the pools and bought his wife a blue fox coat. As they were walking along the road she saw a woman in a white mink.

'Oh George,' she cried, '*that's* what I really wanted.'

'Women!' said George. 'Why didn't you say you wanted a *white* one?'

Ivy: George, quick, wake up! I think that there are burglars in the kitchen! I can hear them eating the pot roast that I made you for dinner!

George: So what are you worrying about? So long as they don't die in the house . . .

An American tourist in Ireland saw a procession led by a priest, a coffin, a man with a muzzled dog and a long line of other men. Intrigued, he walked up to the man with the dog and asked him what was going on.

'It's my wife's funeral procession,' replied the man. 'She died recently.'

'What happened to her?'

'She was savaged by the dog.'

'Can I buy the dog?' asked the American.

'You get in the queue with all the others.'

When Johnny came home from school, his mother asked him how he did in class that day.

'Well,' said Johnny. 'I got O in history, O in geography, O in science, O in arithmetic and O in English.'

When Johnny's father arrived home from work that evening, he asked his wife how Johnny did that day.'

'All right,' she said. 'He got five O levels.'

After serving overseas in the army for two years, a soldier sent a telegram to his wife saying that he was coming home for a fortnight's holiday. But when he arrived home he found no one around. Going upstairs he discovered his wife in bed with another man.

Furious, he raced off to his in-laws and told his wife's father. 'You've got a right daughter, you have. I sent her a telegram telling her that I was coming home after two years, and when I arrive back I find her in bed with another man!'

'I don't believe it,' said the father-in-law.

'Then come and see for yourself.'

They got round to the house and the girl's father went upstairs. A few minutes later he returned, relieved. 'I told you so,' he said. 'She swears by all that's holy she never got the telegram.'

Isaac Goldberg and his wife were invited to a wedding. Isaac, a tailor, was busy, so he told his wife, 'You go to the synagogue and I'll meet you later at the reception.'

But on the day of the wedding he decided that maybe he'd been working too hard and should go to the wedding ceremony after all, and surprise his wife.

On arriving home he found his wife lying naked on the bed, crying.

'What is it my love?' he asked.

'Oh Ikey,' she sobbed. 'I haven't a thing to wear.'

'What?' he said. 'And me in the rag trade? That's ridiculous.' He went over to her wardrobe and opened the door. 'Look in here – you have the red dress, the blue dress, the pink dress, the yellow dress – hello, Sammy – the green dress . . .'

Walking in the cemetery one day Isaac was much moved by the sight of another man sobbing pitifully at a gravestone.

93

'Oh, why did you have to die?' cried the man. 'Why did you have to die?'

Isaac was so touched that he approached the man at the gravestone. 'Are you all right?'

The man continued sobbing and moaning, 'Why, oh why, did you have to die?'

'Was it your mother?' Isaac asked gently.

The man shook his head. 'Why did you have to die?' he wailed.

'Was it your brother?'

Again the man shook his head, still sobbing. 'Why, why did you have to die?'

'Dear me,' said Isaac. 'Then who on earth was it?'

'My wife's first husband.'

Man to friend: My wife has terrible sinus trouble!

Friend: I'm sorry to hear that, pal. How does it affect her?

Man: Every time we go to the shops, she shoves the cheque book under me nose and says 'sign us this' and 'sign us that'!!!

George and Harry were in a pub at the end of the day, and had been there for an hour or so when Harry announced that he was heading off home.

Harry: Well, George, I best be getting off now. You know how the missus gets when I'm late.

George: You want to stick up for yourself more, my son, and be like me – I'm king in my house.

Harry: Yeah, I know. I was there when she crowned you!

After hearing the evidence in a divorce case, the judge delivered his verdict.

'Mrs Smith,' said the judge. 'I have decided to give you five hundred pounds per week.'

'That's very decent of you, your honour,' said her husband. 'When I can afford it, I'll send her something myself!'

George: I just got a beautiful French Peugeot for my wife.
Harry: How come you got such a good trade?

A man came back from the doctor's to give his wife the bad news that he had a dicky heart and would have to pack up work.

'It's all right, darling,' she assured him. 'I can earn some money by streetwalking.' And before he could stop her, she rushed out of the house into the street. Later that night she returned and emptied her purse out on to the bed.

'Five pounds twenty!' said her husband. 'Who on earth gave you twenty pence?'

'Everybody,' she replied.

One fine morning Mr Brown was talking to the new janitor of his block of flats.

'Well, Jack, and how do you like working here?' he asked.

'Oh it's great,' Jack said. 'Everyone's really friendly! And you know, between the two of us, I've made love to every woman in the block – bar one of course!'

On returning to his flat, Mr Brown told his wife about his conversation with Jack. 'And he told me,' said Mr Brown with a laugh, 'that he had made love to every woman in the block except one!'

'Really?' said Mrs Brown thoughtfully. 'Oh, of course. That must be that stuck-up Mrs Smith in number 35!'

During the Second World War, the air sirens went off and Lenny and Ruth were hurriedly getting their things together to rush down to the shelter. They were halfway there when Ruth told her husband she had to go back.

'What on earth for?' said Lenny.

'My teeth,' replied Ruth. 'I can't go down to the shelter without my teeth!'

'Your teeth! You stupid woman, what do you mean, your teeth! They're dropping bombs, not mince pies!'

George was walking awkwardly along a street when he bumped into an old friend.

'Why are you limping?' his friend asked.

'I bought these new shoes the other day and they're killing me.'

'Then why don't you take them back and change them?'

'Because,' said George, 'my wife's being unfaithful to me, my eldest son's spending all my money, my daughter's a drug addict, my second son's in jail and my mother-in-law beats me over the head with a rolling pin whenever she sees me. And if that's not enough, I've got piles. The only pleasure I get is when I take these bloody shoes off.'

Ruby: I am sorry to hear that your father just passed away, Minnie. Did he leave you any money in his will?

Minnie: Not a penny – but he left four thousand pounds for a stone to remember him by.

Ruby: Amazing. Then he didn't leave you that fabulous diamond ring you're wearing, either?

Minnie: No, but that's the stone I bought to remember him by!

Charlie: You look fed up, mate. What's the matter?

Sid: That wife of mine, she's got an allergy.

Charlie: That's a shame. What's she allergic to?

Sid: Fur. Every time she sees a woman in a mink she gets sick.

Sadie was on holiday when she got into conversation with another woman on the beach.

'Good Lord!' she said. 'Look at that boy over there – he's got a crooked mouth, a great big nose and he's cock-eyed!'

'Do you mind?' said the stranger. 'That happens to be my son!'

'Really?' said Sadie. 'And do you know, on him it looks good!'

Two Cockney girls were standing outside a well-known department store.

'Hey Mags,' said one. 'What's that C & A stand for?'
'Fancy not knowing that,' said Mags. 'Coats and 'Ats.'

An American woman to her friend:

'You know, Shirleen, I've been married for forty-seven years and I'm getting a little itchy. How the hell d'you start an affair?'

'Well,' said Shirleen. 'I always say you can't go wrong with the Star Spangled Banner and prawn cocktails.'

On his sixtieth wedding anniversary, Jack was asked by a friend how old his wife was.

'She's eighty-seven and God willing she'll live to be a hundred,' replied Jack.

'And how old are you, Jack?'

'I'm eighty-seven too, but God willing I'll live to be a hundred-and-one.'

'But Jack,' said his friend, 'why do you want to live longer than the wife?'

'To be honest,' said Jack, 'I could do with a year off.'

An old lady sat down next to George on a bus. Presently she turned to him and said, 'You're Jewish, aren't you?'

'No,' said George.

A little while later the old lady turned to him again and said, 'Are you *sure* you're not Jewish?'

'I've told you, madam – I'm not.'

But the old woman was not satisfied, and soon turned to him again. 'Are you positive you're not Jewish?'

'All right, then,' said George. 'I'm Jewish, my life, all ready, oi veh. OK?'

'Funny that,' said the old woman. 'You don't look it.'

Mrs Jones, a widow for some time, decided that she would like a nicer photograph of her dead husband than the one she already had on her dressing-table. So she took the portrait to the photographer in the high street, and asked him to retouch it.

'You see,' she told the photographer, 'in this photo he's wearing a hat. I want you to take off the hat, so I can see his gorgeous hair.'

'I see, madam,' said the photographer. 'And what kind of hair did he have?'

'Well if you take his hat off, you'll find out, won't you?'

Three grandmothers met every week to play cards. One week, another grandmother joined the circle, and the others told her the rules.

'Here,' said the leader, 'we never talk about certain things. One, we don't talk about our children (even though some of them are lawyers or dentists) and we don't talk about our grand-children (even though some of them are in ballet-school) and we *never* talk about sex. For what has gone, has gone.'

A Jewish lady walked up to the palace guard of the Dalai Lama in Tibet, and begged an audience with the holy man. The guard, as he had been instructed, told her that no one was allowed to see the Lama, as the Lama was a hermit and a recluse, devoted to prayer and knowledge of the inward path.

'I don't care,' said the woman. 'I must see the Lama, and speak to him!'

'No one speaks to the Dalai Lama,' replied the guard. 'Or sullies the silent chamber of his devotions.'

'But I only want to say three words to him,' the woman cried. 'Just three words. Is that so terrible? Surely you can let me in to say just three words to him?'

But the palace guard was adamant, and turned the woman away. That night as the palace slept, the woman attempted to get into the courtyard by using a rope and grappling hook – but the palace dogs started barking and alerted the guard.

'Just three words!' she cried, as they carried her away. 'Just three words! You must let me see him!'

But the guards hardened their hearts and threw her back into the street. And so it went on, for three weeks, with the woman constantly begging at the palace gate by day, and trying to get into the temple by stealth at night. Eventually the chief of the palace guard, weakened by lack of sleep, could stand it no more. He went to see the Dalai Lama and arranged an audience for the woman, on the condition that she only said three words. At last she was admitted to the inner sanctum, where the Dalai Lama was sitting on a saffron cushion with his back to her.

'And what are your three words, oh impatient daughter of the West?' he enquired.

'Sidney,' she said. 'Come home.'

7
Hanky Panky

(Love unites)

Sex is probably the most popular topic in the world – look in the papers and it's always in the headlines. So it's a good job we can laugh about it. Of course, to kids, it's a source of endless fascination . . .

One morning in school, Tommy and Johnny were talking about anatomy.

'What d'you reckon is a penis?' asked Tommy.

'I dunno,' said Johnny, 'but I reckon me dad will.'

So that night, Johnny went home and asked his dad to tell him what a penis was. Taking little Johnny aside and ushering him into the bathroom, Johnny's dad took out the article in question and showed his son. 'And that, my boy,' said Johnny's dad, 'is a perfect penis!'

The next day, Tommy was eager to know whatever Johnny had managed to find out from his father. So at break, Johnny took his friend off to the bathroom and there, in one of the cubicles, showed Tommy.

'And if it was two inches shorter,' he said, 'it would be a perfect penis!'

A classroom of schoolchildren were asked for sentences with the word NICE in them. Mary put up her hand and said, 'My daddy bought a new car on Saturday. He took us out into the country and we had a very NICE day.'

'Very good, Mary,' said her teacher. 'Anyone else like to try?'

'Yes, Miss,' said Jimmy. 'My sister came home and told my dad that she was up the spout. "Well," said my dad. "That's nice. That's bloody NICE!"'

Two young boys were talking in the playground at school. Jimmy was admiring Tommy's new watch and asked him where he had got it from.

'Last night I went to the toilet,' said Tommy, 'and saw my mother and father in bed making love. This morning my dad gave me this watch and told me not to say anything about it.'

Jimmy was impressed and decided to do the same as Tommy. That night Jimmy burst into his parents' bedroom and found them making love.

'I want a watch,' he said.

'All right then,' said Jimmy's dad. 'Just sit down in the corner and keep quiet.'

Willie and Fanny were at a swimming pool together.

'Have you got a dog?' asked Willie.

'Yes,' replied Fanny.

'Have you a cat?'

'Yes.'

'Have you a canary?'

'Yes.'

The boy pulled down his swimming trunks. 'But I bet you haven't got one of these!'

The little girl stared at what he was showing off without much enthusiasm. 'My mum says when I'm grown up I can have as many of *those* as I want,' she said.

Two babies were lying in cots in a maternity ward. One turned to the other, and said, 'Hello! What are you – a boy or a girl?'

'I don't know. What are you?'

'I'm a boy.'

'How do you know?'

He lifted up his feet. 'Look – blue bootees!'

Tommy and Jimmy were moaning that they didn't have any pocket money left to go to the pictures. Their friend Johnny overheard.

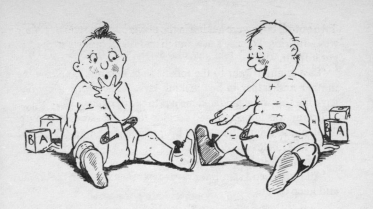

'I know a bloke who'll take you out in his car, take you for a slap-up dinner, take you to the pictures and then run you home all for nothing,' said Johnny.

'Really?' said his friends. 'Did he ask you?'

'No,' said Johnny. 'But he took my sister.'

But of course after a while even sex is mundane . . .

John and Mary were at the zoo looking at the gorilla, when suddenly the gorilla began to be attracted to Mary. He started jumping up and down excitedly. Then he shot an arm through the bars of his cage and began to rip all her clothes off.

'John!' she cried. 'What on earth shall I do?!!'

'What you always do, darling,' he replied nonchalantly. 'Tell him you've got a headache!'

Albert, a regular OAP customer, was looking at the latest headlines in the Sun *about an obscenity trial, when he looked up at me and grinned.*

'I don't know, Maurice,' he said. 'People today get all het up about the young using four-letter words. But it was the same in my day. I remember when I was fourteen, my girlfriend used four-letter words all the time – especially when I got her on the sofa!'

'Really?' I said. 'I can't imagine that. What sort of words were they?'

'Terrible words,' said the old devil, 'like CAN'T, STOP, WON'T!'

After being invalided out of the Navy due to a breakdown a sailor went to see a psychiatrist.

'Now I'm going to show you some sketches and I want you to tell me what they bring to mind,' said the psychiatrist, and he showed the sailor a picture of a train.

'Having sex,' said the sailor.

The psychiatrist showed him a picture of a horse.

'Having sex,' said the sailor.

The psychiatrist then showed him a picture of an elephant.

'Having sex,' said the sailor.

'You're sex mad,' exclaimed the psychiatrist.

'*I'm* sex mad?' said the sailor. 'Who's showing me the dirty pictures?'

From what customers used to tell me, there's life in plenty an old dog yet . . .

Joe, a sixty-five-year-old car dealer, to his young assistant Sid.

Joe: I'm off for the weekend, Joe, taking that gorgeous young receptionist from the King's Head Hotel down to the country. What d'you think of that?

Sid: I think you'll never get your motor started!

Joe: Don't worry, mate, I've thought of that. I've packed a set of jump leads, and you're coming too!

She was only a welder's daughter but she had acetylene legs.

The old man Guiseppe went to see his parish priest.

'Father,' he said. 'I am ninety-two years old and I make love to ten beautiful women every week. What do you think of that?'

'I tell you what I think – I think you're a dirty old man, and that you should pray to the Holy Father for forgiveness.'

'Why should I? I don't believe in God.'

'Then why are you telling me?'

'Why not? I'm telling *everybody*!'

One Sunday night old Bert was sitting in his local when he overheard two young men talking about their wives.

'I took my wife to a show last night,' said one, 'and afterwards we came home and I made love to her six times.'

'Funny that,' said the second man. 'It was my first wedding anniversary yesterday so I took my wife out to see a film and have a slap-up meal. Then I took her home and made love to her six times.'

Bert, married for twenty years, immediately went home. His wife was watching TV, but he switched the set off and said, 'Let's go to bed.'

'Come on,' she replied. 'You're a bit past it now.'

'We'll see who's past it,' Bert told her, and dragged her upstairs.

In bed he made love to her twice, then dozed, made love to her twice again, dozed again, then made love to her two more times. Exhausted by morning, but pleased as punch that he had equalled the record set by the two young men in the pub, he fell into a deep sleep.

At 8.30, he woke up and set off for work with a spring in his step and a gleam in his eye; even though he knew he was late, he decided that it had been worth it.

When he got to the gates of the factory, the foreman hailed him. 'Here, Bert!' he said. 'Where the hell have you been?'

'Oh come on now,' said Bert. 'I haven't been late in thirty-five years. And I'm only an hour late as it is!'

'Yes, *today*,' said the foreman. 'But where were you on Monday and Tuesday?'

Franklin: What's this word propaganda mean?
Desmond: You shore ignorant. Is you married?

Franklin: Yes.
Desmond: How long?
Franklin: Seven year.
Desmond: You got children?
Franklin: No.
Desmond: Well, dat's propaganda.
Franklin: How you mean dat's propaganda?
Desmond: Well, if you bin married seven year an' you ain't go no children, then your wife is the proper goose but you sure ain't the proper gander.

A couple, childless for many years, were sent by their GP to see a famous gynaecologist.

'It seems to me,' said the gynaecologist, 'that you've been trying too hard. You don't have to make love to order, you know. Just do it when the urge comes upon you and perhaps you'll have more success.'

About a year later the gynaecologist was out walking when he came upon the same couple wheeling a pram.

'Congratulations,' he said. 'What happened?'

'Well,' said the proud father. 'It was just as you said. One day we were having a spot of lunch and the urge came upon us and –' he indicated the bouncing baby in the pram.

'Wonderful, wonderful,' said the gynaecologist. 'And were there any complications?'

'Oh no,' said the father. 'Except we've been banned from Macdonalds for life.'

It's when men and women turn into wives and husbands, though, that the fun really starts . . .

John: Let me ask you something, George. Do you like blondes with big blue eyes?
George: Are you mad? Of course I do.
John: Blondes with beautiful high firm white breasts?
George: You bet!
John: And how about girls with lovely long, tapering, athletic legs?

George: Yes, of course.
John: I see. So what are you doing messing around with my wife?

A husband arrived home unexpectedly to find his wife in bed with another man.

'What on earth are you doing?' cried the outraged husband.

'You see?' said the wife to her lover. 'I told you he was stupid.'

A man suspected his wife of being unfaithful but could not catch her in the act. So one morning, after pretending to go to work, he sneaked back into the bedroom and hid behind a screen, armed with a camera.

Sure enough, half an hour later a man arrived and got into bed with his wife. As the couple made love, the husband photographed them in various positions from behind the screen.

The next day the husband confronted the lover with the developed films.

'Well?' he demanded. 'What have you got to say about these?'

'They're very good,' said the lover. 'Can I have six large and two small of each?'

Returning to work after lunch one day a man said to his friend, 'You know, Fred, I've got a funny feeling that my wife is up to something. Whenever I go home for lunch she looks a bit dishevelled, and I'm getting suspicious.'

'What time do you normally go for lunch?' asked Fred.

'About half past twelve.'

'Tell you what – why don't you go home at twelve o'clock tomorrow?'

The man agreed, and went home early the next day. When he returned to work Fred asked him what had happened.

'I went upstairs,' he said, 'and found her in bed with another man.'

'What did you do?'

'I went back downstairs and made some lunch for myself.'

'What about the other man?'

'He can make his own bloody lunch.'

Harry was making love to a woman when her husband unexpectedly returned. He leapt out of the window and, spotting some joggers running by, joined them.

'Do you usually jog in the nude?' one of the runners asked after a while.

'Oh yes,' said Harry. 'It's very invigorating.'

'And do you usually jog with a condom on?'

Harry went red, but kept his head. 'Well, to tell you the truth,' he said, 'it was raining when I set out.'

A man having problems with his sex life was advised by his doctor to jog four miles a day.

'Well?' asked the doctor, after a week had elapsed. 'How did it go?'

'How should I know?' came the reply. 'I was twenty-eight miles away.'

Late at night, a drunk was trying to open the door of his house when he was approached by a policeman.

'What exactly are you doing, sir?' he asked.

'Trying to get into my house, ossifer.'

Seeing that the man was very drunk – in fact, incapable – the constable was cautious. 'And how do I know it's your house, sir?'

'Here's the keys,' said the drunk. 'Try them yourself.'

The keys fitted, and the two men entered the house. The drunk proved very proud of the place, and insisted on giving the policeman a guided tour.

'This is the lounge,' he began, 'and this is the kitchen, and this is the living room and this is the hallway.' They climbed the stairs.

Opening the bedroom door, the drunk continued without pause, 'And this is the bedroom, this is my bed, that lady is my wife and that man next to her is – that's me!'

Men are always saying their wives don't understand them. With some men it's a wonder anyone understands them!

A very naïve man came home late and rather drunk, and ran into his son on the way up the stairs.

Father: Here, son. Don't tell your mother, but I've just joined a prostitutes club! Look – they gave me a card!

Son: Dad, what is the matter with you? This doesn't say prostitutes club, it says parachute club!

Father: Oh, no. And they guaranteed me three hundred and sixty-five jumps a year!

A Jew was sitting opposite a priest on a train.

'Tell me,' said the Jew to the priest. 'Why do you wear your collar back to front?'

'I'm a father,' said the priest.

'I'm a father, too,' said the Jew. 'But I don't wear my collar back to front.'

'You don't understand, my son. I'm a father of thousands.'

'In that case,' said the Jew. 'You'd have been better off wearing your trousers back to front.'

Jock went out to celebrate Hogmanay and, as is usual on such occasions, after imbibing enough alcohol to fell an ox, he ended up fast asleep in the middle of the main road in the early hours of the morning. Passing him on their way to work, two shop girls, Mary and Jessie, were curious as to what a Scotsman wore beneath the tartan. So they lifted up the kilt to reveal his nether regions in all their naked glory. Mary, being a modest type, decided that they could not leave him so exposed to the elements. So she took a red ribbon from her bag and tied a large bow on the Scotsman's pride and joy. Then she and Jessie, giggling, continued on their way.

When Jock woke up later he was seized by the call of nature, and dashing round the corner he lifted his kilt to the wall. Then he saw the bow.

'Well laddie,' he said to himself. 'I'm reet proud of you. I dinna ken where ye wair last night, but wherever it was, ye won first prize!'

A young army officer arrived at his new HQ to be welcomed by his CO. After showing the boy round the camp, the CO outlined the recreational activities on offer.

CO: Well, Cameron, on Mondays we have a snooker tournament. Very jolly. Everyone pays a pound, and the winner takes the pot.

Cameron: I'm afraid I don't play snooker, sir.

CO: Really? Oh well, you'll like Tuesdays – Tuesday nights we have a darts match. First one to three-hundred-and-one, a little side bet, a few drinks . . .

Cameron: Sorry sir. I don't like gambling, and I can't play darts.

CO: Oh. Well, on Wednesday nights a few young girls come up from the village for a dance – bit of hanky panky, all good clean fun, of course . . .

Cameron: Sorry, sir, but I don't have no time for women.

CO: Good god, man. You're not *GAY* are you?

Cameron: Certainly not, sir.

CO: Oh dear. Then you're not going to like Thursday and Friday nights much, either.

A driver gave a lift to a very attractive young girl in Whitechapel. After looking at her in the mirror for some time he turned to her and said, 'You have the eyes of an angel.'

'Thank you,' said the girl.

'And a pair of legs like a ballerina's.'

'That's very kind of you.'

'And you've got the breasts of a goddess.'

'Really?' she said. 'Would you like to see where I got my appendix scar?'

'Yes,' said the eager driver.

'Over there,' said the girl, pointing through the window. 'In the London Hospital.'

A young insurance man called on a house and found the front door open. He walked inside, and there, in the living room, a beautiful blonde was breast-feeding her baby.

For a while the young man was totally taken aback, and all he could do was stand and stare at the scene with his mouth wide open. When she saw him the blonde laughed.

'What on earth's the matter with you?' she said. 'Haven't you ever seen this sort of thing before?'

'N-no,' stammered the boy. 'I was an only child.'

Putting the baby down into its cot, she came towards him. 'Would you like to try it?' she asked throatily.

The young lad quickly agreed, and taking her left breast in his mouth, began to suck greedily.

'Don't neglect the other one,' she said. So he took out her left breast and replaced it with the right one.

Amorously, the blonde bent her head close to his ear and whispered, 'Is there anything else you'd like?'

The young man looked up blissfully and asked, 'You haven't got a dry biscuit, have you?'

Of course not all men want a woman on a long-term arrangement. Sometimes just one night is enough . . .

An Irishman went with a Jewish prostitute one night. The experience was pretty unsatisfactory for them both.

'Huh!' he said. 'I thought all Jews were supposed to be tight!'

'Yes,' she replied. 'And I thought all Irishmen were supposed to be thick!'

Ted was on holiday in Munich, when a lady of easy virtue approached him.

'Hello darling,' she purred. 'How would you like to come home with me?'

'How much do you charge?' he asked cautiously.

'Fifty marks.'

'American Express?'

'Darling,' she said. 'I don't care how fast you go!!'

The following morning, Ted was ready to leave when she called him back.

'*Mein herr*,' said the lady. 'Haff you forgotten my marks?'

'Oh I'm sorry,' said the man. 'Eight out of ten.'

Cross an elephant with a call-girl and you get a three ton pick-up.

Ted was in a bar when he was propositioned by the barmaid. 'Come to my flat tonight,' she told him, 'and I'll show you a good time. It's really exotic.'

'How's that?' asked Ted.

'I've got mirrors on the floor, mirrors on the walls and mirrors on the ceiling.' She winked. 'Come around tonight after time and bring a bottle with you.'

The man arrived at eleven o'clock. The barmaid opened the door wearing nothing but a long black negligee and a dab of perfume. She led him inside.

'Did you bring a bottle?' she asked him breathlessly.

Ted took out the bottle from his carrier bag.

'What the bloody hell is this?' said the woman. 'It's pink!'

'It's always that colour,' said Ted. 'It's Windolene.'

A man went to the Bunny Club in Piccadilly and asked to speak to Anna Rose, a stunning brunette who worked as a croupier there. When she appeared he took her aside and said, 'I won't beat about the bush. You are a beautiful young woman, and if you agree to come out with me tonight, have a meal, go to a show and then spend the night at my place I'll give you two hundred pounds.'

'Two hundred pounds?' she said. 'Do you mean it?'

'Yes,' he said. 'I'll even give you a hundred up front.'

So she agreed to go out with him, and at the end of the night he paid her the full two hundred pounds.

The following night he turned up again and the same thing happened: he offered her two hundred pounds to go out with him and spend the night at his place. Again she agreed and was paid. The third night the same thing happened, but after they made love and he'd paid her another two hundred pounds, he told her that he wouldn't be seeing her again.

'Why not?' she asked, disappointed, and having enjoyed being so well paid for her services.

'I'm going home to Tel Aviv in the morning,' he told her.

'Tel Aviv?' she said. 'What a coincidence. My brother lives there.'

'I know,' he said. 'He gave me the six hundred quid to give you.'

A girl in a bus queue had difficulty in getting on to the bus because of the tightness of her dress. So she undid the bottom three buttons at the back of the dress. Then she felt herself being lifted bodily on to the platform by the man standing behind her.

'Thank you very much,' she said. 'You didn't have to do that.'

'I did,' said the man. 'They were my buttons you were undoing.'

Neil, a young bachelor, moved into a new flat and invited a friend around for a drink.

'Kim,' he said. 'It's a lonely place, but there are compensations. Opposite there's a fantastic view. Through the window I can see a beautiful girl undressing every day.'

Kim went to the window, 'Funny,' he said. 'I can't see anything.'

'Yes, well,' said Neil. 'You can if you move the dressing table, get that stool and stand it on this table.'

She was only a jockey's daughter but all the horse manure.

Jones and Brown had farms close to one another. Jones had a daughter called Mary, and Brown had a son called Charlie. Charlie and Mary became very friendly and eventually Charlie put Mary in the family way. When Mary told her father the news he was furious, and marched off to see Mr Brown.

'Your son's given my daughter a baby,' he yelled. 'What do you think of that?'

'That son of mine's a clumsy bugger,' Brown replied. 'He broke a shovel this morning.'

Birds do it, bees do it, even Pekinese do it . . .

A prawn fell in love with a crab, so she went to tell her family.

'I'm in love with a crab and I want to marry him,' she told them.

'Marry a crab!' said her father. 'You can't marry a crab! They walk sideways! It's unthinkable! I won't hear of it!'

The poor prawn went unhappily back to the crab to tell him of her father's decision. But the crab simply told her that on that Sunday he would come to see her father and make him change his mind. That Sunday, all the prawns were sitting around in the rock pool, when the crab walked in and, advancing in a beautiful straight line towards her father, asked for the prawn's feeler in marriage.

'Oh, crab!' cried the prawn in delight. 'You're walking straight!'

'Quiet!' hissed the crab. 'I'm pissed.'

A farmer had a parrot, and one day, as he was going off to market, he put the parrot in the back of the van and set off to buy some chickens. On the way home, the farmer suddenly realized that all the chickens were out of their cages and walking down the road after the van, while the parrot sat in state in the back, squawking after them, 'Any time you change your minds, girls, you can get back in the van and ride!'

But everyone likes it in the open air . . . !

A man was walking down a country lane with a bucket balanced on his head, a pig under one arm and a chicken under the other, when he realized that he had lost his way. Coming upon Molly, a pretty young country wench, he asked her the way to the market.

'Well,' said Molly. 'I'm a-going that very way myself, sir. But I dursen't walk along with you, for you might take advantage of me.'

Taken aback, the young man replied, 'And how the devil could I do that, seeing as I've a bucket balanced on me head, a pig under one arm and a chicken under the other?'

'Well,' said Molly softly. 'If you put the chicken in the bucket, I could always hold the pig for you.'

'The British must be the healthiest nation in the world – why else would they close all the hospitals?'

8
Hair Today, Gone Tomorrow

(Keeping in trim)

None of us is getting any younger, but when people ask me how I am, I just give them a grin full of false teeth and recall the old rhyme . . .

I'm Fine Thanks

There is nothing the matter with me. I'm as healthy as I can be.
I have arthritis in both knees and when I talk I talk with a wheeze.
My pulse is weak and my blood is thin but I'm awfully good for the shape I'm in.

Arch supports I have for my feet, or I wouldn't be able to be on the street.
Sleep is denied me every night, but every morning I find I'm alright.
My memory's failing, my head's in a swim, but I'm awfully good for the shape I'm in.

The moral is this, as this tale I unfold, that for you and for me that are growing old,
It's better to say 'I'm fine' with a grin, than let folks know the shape we are in.
How do I know that my youth is all spent? Well, my get-up-and-go has got up and went.
But I don't really mind, when I think with a grin of all the grand places my get-up has been.

Old age is golden, I've heard it said, but sometimes I wonder as I get into bed.

With my ears in a drawer, my teeth in a cup, my eyes on the table
   for when I wake up.
'Ere sleep comes to me I say to myself, is there anything else I
   should lay on the shelf?

I get up each morning and dust off my wits: pick up the paper
   and read the obits. If my name is still missing, I know I'm not
   dead, so I get a good breakfast and go back to bed.

*A barber should always help his customers out when he can – so when a
Polish customer came in to the shop and called me madam, I told him
he needed his eyes tested! He obviously hadn't been in the country long,
so I told him he could get spectacles free on the National Health and
gave him the address of a friend of mine who was a reliable optician.*
   The Pole duly made an appointment with the optician, who
asked him to read the bottom line of his eye chart.
   'Read it?' said the Pole. 'I know him!'

The optician eventually retired after a very successful career, and
members of his profession gave a dinner in his honour. After a
sumptuous meal he was presented with the portrait of an eye as
a memento of his work. The optician, much moved, rose to give
his speech of thanks.
   'I shall cherish this portrait of an eye,' he told them, 'happy in
the thought that I was not a gynaecologist.'

A tramp went to a doctor for a check-up.
   'Get undressed,' the doctor told him.
   The tramp took his clothes off.
   'I'm not examining you,' said the doctor. 'You're too filthy to
be touched. Get out of here.'
   The tramp put on his clothes again and left. He went to
another doctor and asked to be examined. This doctor also told
him to get undressed, so he stripped off again.

'I'm not examining you,' the doctor said. 'You're too filthy to be touched.'

'Funny,' said the tramp. 'That's what the last doctor told me.'

'Then why did you come here?'

'I wanted a second opinion.'

A health inspector at a mental home stopped to talk to one of the inmates. The man proved to be friendly and articulate, and the health inspector was very favourably impressed.

'You shouldn't be in here,' he said. 'Tell me, what did you do in the outside world?'

'I was a bricklayer,' said the inmate.

'Well, I'm going to do my very best to get you out of here and back into society.'

As the inspector turned to leave, a brick came flying through the air and hit him squarely on the back of his head. Just before he lost consciousness he saw the face of the inmate looming over him.

'You won't forget, will you?'

In a barber's everyone talks about their health – we're a nation of hypochondriacs. Mind you, some have more reason to worry than others . . .

One of my customers told me that he was going to see a specialist.

'How did you get on?' I asked him the next time he came in for a shave.

'I'm worried. He told me to take one pill a day for the rest of my life.'

'That's not so bad,' I said.

'He only gave me three.'

George bumped into his old friend Harry on the street.

'Harry!' he said. 'I never thought I'd see you again. I heard that your doctor only gave you six months.'

'He did,' said Harry. 'But when I couldn't pay his bill he gave me another six months.'

Of course some people have only themselves to blame if they're sick.

A man, seriously ill in hospital, was visited by his business partner, Jack.

'Jack,' the man gasped. 'I know I haven't got long to live so I'm going to make a confession to you. Remember that time your Jaguar was nicked and smashed up?'

'Yes,' said Jack.

'That was no ordinary thief, Jack. It was me. I took it for a joy-ride and when I pranged it, I ran away before the police came.'

'I know,' said Jack.

'And Jack? You know that ten thousand quid of yours that went missing from the bank?' croaked the stricken man. 'I embezzled it.'

'I know,' said Jack.

'And the fancy man who's been playing around with your wife behind your back?' cried the man. 'It was me all along!'

'I know,' said Jack.

'You knew all this and yet you've done nothing?'

'I did something,' said Jack. 'I poisoned you.'

A man went to see his doctor and told him that he was constipated. When the doctor asked him about his diet, the man told him that he ate only snooker balls.

'What did you have for breakfast?' asked the doctor.

'Two reds and a blue,' said the man.

'And what did you have for lunch?'

'Three reds, a pink, a white and a brown.'

'And for dinner?'

'Four reds, a yellow and a black.'

'You know what the problem is,' said the doctor. 'You aren't getting enough greens.'

And you can't be too careful when it comes to hygiene . . .

A man went into a chemist's and saw a notice saying: CONTRACEPTIVES FITTED HERE.

He asked the assistant, 'Do you fit contraceptives?'

'Yes,' she replied.

'Then wash your hands and get me a quarter of cough drops.'

For years Mrs Cohen was discontented with her physique. Then one day she saw an advertisement in a newspaper that offered her exactly the sort of figure she wanted, and which involved a very expensive course of hormone treatment. She decided it was worth it and wrote off for the course. A few weeks later she went to her doctor.

'Mrs Cohen,' he said. 'You look marvellous – at last you'll be able to go to dances, wear all the latest fashions, eat at smart restaurants, wear a bikini –'

'I can't wear a bikini,' she interrupted.

'Why not?'

She opened the front of her dress and to the doctor's horror, her chest and belly were covered with dark curly hair.

'Good grief,' said the doctor. 'How far down does the hair go?'

'All the way to my balls.'

And it's not just patients who worry . . .

A man went to visit his doctor.

'I haven't seen you in a long time,' said the doctor.

'No,' said the man, 'I've been ill.'

'Don't tell me,' said the doctor. 'Have you been wheezing, coughing, can't sleep?'

'Yes,' said the man.

'Funny that,' said the doctor. 'So have I. I wonder what it is?'

A man was sitting, first in line, in the waiting room at his doctor's. A black man entered and went straight past the queue and into the surgery.

'Here, wait a minute,' said the first man. 'I was here first and I'm white.'

'I don't care what colour you are,' said the black man. 'I'm the doctor.'

A man was telling a friend about his son-in-law.

'He's an amazing doctor!' he said. 'He's been treating a patient for the last twenty years for jaundice – and he's just found out that he's Chinese!'

'That *is* amazing,' said his friend.

'I'll say,' said the man. 'He cured him!'

Then there are always those who are looking for nothing short of a miracle . . .

A man went to the doctor – he was sixty-five – and asked him if there was any way to increase his sex life.

'Well,' said the doctor. 'I can give you an injection, but I can't promise anything – so there's no charge.'

However, after the injection, the patient insisted on giving the doctor a five pound note. Two weeks later, the old man returned, requested another injection and then forced a ten pound note into the doctor's hand.

'Why the extra five pounds?' asked the doctor.

'That's from the wife.'

A man of seventy-five went to the doctor.

'Look,' he explained to the GP. 'This may surprise you, but I've got a date with a twenty-five-year-old girl. Do you think you could give me something to pep me up a bit?'

The doctor gave him some medicine and the old boy went happily away. That evening the doctor was so curious to know how the old man got on that he telephoned him at home.

'Well?' he asked. 'Did it work?'

'Not half,' replied the old boy gleefully. 'Seven times!'

'Good lord!' said the doctor. 'And what about your young lady?'

'Oh, I don't know, doctor. She hasn't turned up yet!'

Ted went to the doctor with an upset stomach.

'Are you regular?' asked the doctor.

'Oh, yes,' said Ted. 'That's the problem – I go every morning at eight o'clock.'

'Splendid. What's wrong with that?'

'I don't get up till half past eight.'

After being examined by her doctor, a woman returned home to her husband.

'You know, Tom,' she said. 'Dr Stevenson said I have the figure of a twenty-five-year-old girl!'

'Oh yeah?' laughed Tom. 'What about your big bum?'

'Actually,' she replied. 'He didn't mention you!'

Two brothers went to see their doctor together, each with a delicate problem.

'And what exactly seems to be the trouble?' the doctor asked them.

The brothers stared at the doctor with embarrassment and hesitated before finally explaining.

It emerged that the elder brother, George, had a penis which was far too large, while his brother, Jack, had the opposite problem – he was hopelessly under-equipped.

The doctor examined them both and was able to confirm their respective stories.

'You're in luck,' he told them, then explained that there were new pills on the market which could alter the size of the male appendage. Blue pills would make a penis bigger, while red ones would reduce its size. He wrote out their prescriptions and told them to come back in a week's time.

A week later, Jack burst into the surgery. 'Doctor, doctor these pills are useless!' the poor man cried, slamming the bottle of pills on the doctor's table. 'Look at this!' And taking down his trousers, he displayed himself – what there was of it to display.

'My god!' said the doctor. 'You've been taking the red pills! Where on earth is George?'

'He's outside, doctor. Unloading his off a lorry.'

A man went to the doctor's with terrible pains in his ears.

'I'm afraid that you'll have to have your dick removed,' the doctor told him.

'Well,' the man replied. 'I can't bear this pain any more, so I suppose I'll just have to have it taken off.'

Two days later the man went to his tailor, who asked him which way he wanted the trousers to hang.

'Oh,' said the man, 'I don't care. It doesn't really matter, does it?'

'It certainly does,' replied the tailor. 'If they don't hang right you get terrible pains in your ears!'

Old Mr Thompson went to the doctor.
Patient: I'm having terrible trouble passing water, Doctor.
Doctor: I see. And how old are you, Mr Thompson?
Patient: Ninety-two.
Doctor: Oh well, you've peed enough.

Of course, doctors are always telling us 'it's all in the mind' – but sometimes they're undoubtedly right – take this conversation I over-heard for instance . . .

'I say, old boy, you look a bit under the weather.'

'Well, old chap, I have been a bit run down lately, I must admit. I went to see my psychiatrist and do you know, the feller told me I was in love with my umbrella!'

'In love with your umbrella? Preposterous!'

'Absolutely! The man's a fool. Everyone knows we're just good friends.'

Mrs Cohen went to her doctor after suffering a week or more of strange stomach pains. The doctor examined her and told her that she was pregnant.

'PREGNANT? But doctor, I'm seventy-nine, and my husband's eighty-four! It's impossible!' wailed Mrs Cohen.

'Well I'm sorry, Mrs Cohen, but facts are facts. All the tests show that you are expecting a baby,' replied the doctor.

She was so shocked that without waiting to get home, she telephoned her husband and told him the amazing news.

'Brace yourself, Willie,' she said. 'The doctor's just told me that I'm pregnant.'

'Good god!' said Willie. 'And who is this speaking, please?'

A man went to his doctor with a frog in his ear.

'How on earth did that happen?' asked the doctor.

'It used to be wart on my foot,' said the frog.

Patient to psychiatrist: Everyone takes advantage of me – I just can't seem to stick up for myself.

Psychiatrist: Don't let it worry you.

Patient: How much do I owe you?

Psychiatrist: How much have you got, shorty?

My son is a famous surgeon. He's a genius. If you're at death's door, he'll pull you through.

I don't know anyone who actually likes going to the dentist, but Sadie really dreaded it. Mind you, with the clumsy chap she used to go to, it was hardly surprising . . .

Sadie was in the dentist's chair, white as a sheet and shaking all over.

Dentist: What's the matter? I haven't even started drilling yet!

Sadie: I know! You're standing on my corns!

After that start, you'd think he'd mind his manners, wouldn't you? But not a bit of it . . .

Dentist: You know this tooth is dreadfully decayed. I'm afraid it will have to come out.

Sadie: Oh no! Oh, goodness, I'd rather have a baby!

Dentist (with a leer): Well make up your mind. I can always adjust the chair!

Another time Sadie went to the same dentist and was given gas. When she woke the dentist told her, 'I took three teeth out.'

'Three?' she said. 'I only came in for two extractions.'

'I know,' said the dentist, 'but I gave you too much gas and I didn't want to waste it.'

Things don't even get any better when you've had all the darn things out . . .

A man had been told by his dentist that his new teeth wouldn't be ready for three weeks.

Man: Three weeks! What on earth am I supposed to do until then?

Dentist: Well, you could always be an advert for Rowntree's clear gums!

Sid went to his dentist to have a new set of teeth made. After examination, he was told that they would cost him eight hundred pounds. Deciding that this was a bit stiff, to say the least, he thought he would try somebody else. After examination by the second dentist, he was told that the new set would only cost him two hundred pounds.

'Two hundred pounds!' Sid exclaimed. 'That sounds incredibly cheap – I've just been quoted eight hundred up the road for the same work – I can't believe that your job could be very good at that price.'

'Well,' said the dentist, 'if you want to know what sort of job I do you'd better ask someone who's got a set of my teeth already.'

'Well, who would you suggest?' asked Sid, but before the dentist could reply, a little man came in and paid his bill. Deciding to ask him for an unbiased opinion, the man followed the little man into a tailor's shop just over the road from the second dentist's surgery.

'I was wondering if you could help me,' asked Sid. 'I believe that you had a set of dentures made at the surgery across the road, and I'd like you to tell me what they're like before I get a set made myself.'

'It's incredible,' said the tailor. 'What a life I have had. Do you know how old I am? Take a close look, come on – what would you say? Fifty-four? Fifty-five? No, you won't believe me. I'm sixty-five. My wife now, Rosie, she was the same, young to the grave, God rest her soul, went when she was seventy-two – but me, now –'

'Yes, well this is all very interesting,' said Sid, 'but what I really want to know is –'

'And we had such perfect children,' interrupted the tailor. 'Martin, what a boy – apple of his mother's eye, he was. But my little Rosie, she is my favourite. A jewel, married to such a nice boy – a doctor – they live out of London now, of course, a beautiful house just south of Bromley –'

'Look, this is fascinating, really, but what about your teeth?'

'And when I go down to their place,' continued the old man, 'you would think I was the king! My own room, hot showers, good food, anything I like! It's like being on holiday! Swimming pool, I can swim there any time I like.'

'Your teeth?' Sid tried feebly.

'I love to swim, wonderful exercise. And the last time I was down there it was fantastic. As I was doing the backstroke, I saw the most beautiful young girl coming towards me, dressed only in one of those little things, you know, bikinis? And she looked me up and down and said, "Excuse me, but do you always bathe in the nude?" Because I do, you see. It is so good for the circulation – and I said –'

'If I could just ask you, please!' Sid broke in desperately, 'I want to know about your *teeth*!'

'And I said, "Ach, yes, it is so good for the circulation", and at that, she took off even her tiny little bikini-thing, you know, and dived into the pool with me. Before I knew it, she was tickling me and fondling my intimate parts and kissing me all over, and breathing in my ear –'

'WHAT ABOUT YOUR TEETH!'

'MY TEETH!' said the old man. 'I'll tell you about my teeth! That's the first time in six months these bloody teeth haven't hurt me at all!'

Will there be anything else, sir?

Maurice Lautman was a full-time professional hairdresser for over forty years in the East End of London, where his inexhaustible supply of jokes and anecdotes made his barber's shop a popular haunt for anyone who liked to laugh.

His talent for entertaining people, he believes, was inherited from his late father, Benjamin Lautman, who in his time was 'a great dancer', and all the Lautman boys, Sam, Nat, Maurice and Mark have enjoyed the limelight on an amateur basis throughout their lives, whether singing, dancing or, naturally, telling jokes, while sticking to their 'day jobs' as hairdressers.

Maurice has now retired from hairdressing and lives with his wife Edna and daughter Louise in North London.